HANDLIST OF
MUSIC MANUSCRIPTS
ACQUIRED 1908–67

HANDLIST OF
MUSIC
MANUSCRIPTS
ACQUIRED
1908–67

PAMELA J. WILLETTS

ASSISTANT KEEPER
DEPARTMENT OF MANUSCRIPTS

PUBLISHED BY THE TRUSTEES OF
THE BRITISH MUSEUM
1970

Printed in Great Britain by
Alden & Mowbray Ltd
at the Alden Press, Oxford

PREFACE

THIS handlist of the music manuscripts acquired since the publication of Augustus Hughes-Hughes's *Catalogue of Manuscript Music in the British Museum*, 3 vols., 1906–1909 (reprinted 1964–1966) is intended as a stopgap until a detailed catalogue can be produced. It has been prepared by Miss Pamela J. Willetts, Assistant Keeper in the Department, with assistance in compiling the index from Mr. P. H. Cadell, formerly Assistant Keeper in the Department.

The handlist covers accessions of manuscript music up to the end of 1967. The descriptions are summary but the date and content of each item are indicated; for fuller information about the Additional and Egerton MSS. reference should be made to the relevant volumes of the *Catalogue of Additions*, of which that for 1936–1945 is at present in the press. Letters of composers have also been included so far as possible. All composers mentioned in the descriptions are included in the index, but the sources before 1700 have been more fully treated; for example, every composer mentioned in the Tregian Anthology, Egerton MS. 3665, is indexed. Some collections are of very recent acquisition and it is possible that when detailed cataloguing of these is undertaken some reassignment of the reference numbers may have to be made. Details of manuscripts *on loan* are correct at the time of going to press but are, of course, subject to alteration.

The summary list of the music manuscripts preserved with printed music in the Music Room has been prepared by Mr. O. W. Neighbour, Assistant Keeper in the Department of Printed Books.

T. C. SKEAT
Keeper of Manuscripts

7 January 1969

CONTENTS

PREFACE   v

ADDITIONAL MANUSCRIPTS   1

EGERTON MANUSCRIPTS   69

MUSIC MANUSCRIPTS ON LOAN
    to the Department of Manuscripts   76

MUSIC MANUSCRIPTS
    preserved with printed collections in
    the Music Room, Department of
    Printed Books   86

INDEX   99

ADDITIONAL MANUSCRIPTS

1908

37772. MISCELLANEOUS VOLUME:

L (1). Johann Heinrich Viktor Rose: eight keyboard variations on Paisiello's 'Nel cor più non mi sento'; late 18th cent. ff. 59–62b.

(2). Friedrich Ludwig Schrödl: two sonatas for violoncello and bass;
late 18th cent. ff. 63–70.

Q. Three canzonettas for solo voice and bass, etc., and one duet; before
1782? (date and initials 'M.B.' to first and last item). ff. 90–2b.

U (1). 'J.V.': cantata, 'Spirits Revels'; 'July 1805'. ff. 104–7.

(2). Canzonetta, 'Solitario bosco ombroso'; early 19th cent. ff. 108, 108b.

1909

37779. AGOSTINO STEFFANI: twelve duets with a bass, followed by two attributed in other manuscripts to Carlo Luigi Pietragrua; *circ.* 1700.

37781–3. SIR JULIUS BENEDICT: opera, 'The Lily of Killarney'; copied by John
Cornwall, 1898–1900. Full score.

1910

37956–64. ÉDOUARD SILAS: *autograph* scores. As follows:

37956–7. 'Joash', sacred drama; 1858.

37958–60. 'Nitocris', grand opera; 1859.

37961. Symphony in A, op. 19; 1852.

37962. Symphony in C, op. 96; 1876.

37963. 'Mr Punch's Musical Recollections', burlesque symphony;
1856–66.

37964. 'Elegie', op. 34, 1856, and 'March of Vagabonds', op. 90, 1873.

Bequeathed by the composer.

37968. LIBRETTO (based on a comedy by Goldoni) for the opera, 'La Donna di
Genio Volubile', by Marcos Antonio Portogallo; *circ.* 1800?

Transferred from the Department of Printed Books.

37976. ALESSANDRO SCARLATTI: opera, 'L'Olimpia Vendicante'; late 17th cent. Score.

37995. LIBRETTO by G. Palomba for the opera, 'Amore vince tutto . . . ', by Pietro Carlo Guglielmi; '9 Giugno 1810 Padova'.

37999. MISCELLANEOUS VOLUME:
ff. 66–7b. J. Bourne: mock lecture at the Oxford Music School, addressed to women; 1642.

38002. GEORGE FRIDERIC HANDEL: opera, 'Admeto'; copied by John Christopher Smith, mid 18th cent. Full score.

38036. CANTATAS by Legnani, Bencini, Sarro, Lotti, Caldara, Bononcini, Conti, Torri, Monari, Ariosti, Fago, Mancini, Tosi, Martini, A. Scarlatti, Albinoni; 1706.

38057. CHARLES FRANÇOIS GOUNOD: motet, 'O Salutaris Hostia'; 'Janvier, 1856'. Full score. *Autograph.*

38058. ANDRÉ GEORGES LOUIS ONSLOW: First Symphony, op. 41; before 1830. Full score.

38068–72. MORTEN COLLECTION. Music manuscripts collected by Alfred Morten; 18th–19th cent. As follows:
38068. Johann Sebastian Bach: Prelude and Fugue in G (no. 15 of *Das Wohltemperirte Clavier*, Part II); mid 18th cent.
38069. Miscellaneous music:
(1). George Frideric Handel: cantata, 'Qualor l'egre Pupille'; 18th cent. ff. 1–4b.
(2). Franz Joseph Haydn: title-page of *VI Original Canzonettas* [1794], with the signature of the composer. ff. 5, 5b.
(3). Charles Simon Catel: 'Quatuor énigmatique . . . fait pour Cherubini le 15 avril, 1811'. *Autograph.* ff. 6–7.
(4). Ludwig van Beethoven: canon, 'Ars longa Vita brevis'; after 1825. ff. 8–9.
(5). Richard Wagner: first violin part of the overture, 'Polonia'; after 1832. ff. 10–14b.
(6). Dr. George William Chard: Psalm 41, 'Happy the man, whose tender care', arranged from an air by Bellini for four voices with organ; before 1849. ff. 15–17b.

38070. Miscellaneous music:

(1). Giovanni Battista Pergolesi?: 'Miserere à nove voci'; 18th cent. ff. 1–25b.

(2). Giuseppe Scolari: aria, 'Già la Morte in mante nero', for tenor and orchestra; 18th cent. ff. 26–41b.

(3). Wolfgang Amadeus Mozart?: fragment ($2\frac{1}{4}$ bars) for orchestra (not in Köchel); late 18th cent. f. 42.

(4). Molto Andante in D minor (16 bars) for keyboard in the same hand as (3). f. 42b.

(5). Johann Georg Albrechtsberger: four canons; 18th cent. *Autograph?* ff. 44–5b.

(6). Carl Friedrich Zelter: motet, 'Tenebrae factae sunt'; 18th–19th cent. *Autograph.* ff. 46–9b.

(7). Niccolò Antonio Zingarelli: motet, 'Tantum ergo'; 18th–19th cent. *Autograph?* ff. 50, 50b.

(8). Ludwig van Beethoven: sketch for the Andante of op. 131; 1826. *Autograph.* ff. 51–2b.

(9). William Crotch: arrangement of the overture and part of Scene I of Grétry's opera, 'Zémire et Azor': 1804. *Autograph.* ff. 53–6.

(10). Gottfried Weber: musical *autograph*; Mainz, 25 Oct. 1818. f. 57.

(11). Johann Baptist Cramer: two keyboard variations on 'Rule Britannia'; early 19th cent. *Autograph.* ff. 58–9.

(12). Johann Sebastian Bach: 'Sebastian Bach's Trios', i.e. the Six Sonatas 'à 2 Clav. e Pedal' (BWV 525–530); early 19th cent. ff. 60–75b.

(13). Three short pieces arranged for pianoforte in the same hand as (12). ff. 76–7.

(14). Giovanni Pierluigi da Palestrina: three motets à 4 copied by Abbé Fortunato Santini; early 19th cent.

(15). Benedetto Marcello: two madrigals; early 19th cent. ff. 84–94b.

(16). Edward Wolff: Nocturne in G minor for pianoforte: early 19th cent. ff. 95–7.

38071. Letters of musicians including: Haydn, Hummel, Beethoven (receipt), Samuel Wesley, Spontini, Mercadante, Meyerbeer, Gottfried Weber, Schumann, Mendelssohn, Spohr, Czerny, Clara Schumann, Gounod, Joachim, Sullivan, and others.

38072. Portraits of musicians (mainly *engraved*) including Bach, Handel, C. P. E. Bach, Mozart, Mendelssohn, Schumann.

Presented by Mrs. Clara Morten in accordance with the wishes of her late husband, Alfred Morten, Esq.

38091. MISCELLANEOUS VOLUME:

E. Felix Mendelssohn Bartholdy: two letters to William Bartholomew and note of metronome times in 'Elijah'; Leipzig, 3, 18 July 1846. ff. 45–9.

Presented by Mrs. L. J. Edwards in memory of her husband, Frederick George Edwards.

1911

38163. LIST OF SONGS for the lute, etc., including 'Nowellys', 'O admyrabile', 'Reges Tharsys', etc.; 15th cent. Written on the back of a roll (1397) recording acts of John Colton, Archbishop of Armagh.

38176–7. HENRY FESTING JONES: music dramas, 'Narcissus' and 'Ulysses', to words by Samuel Butler; 1887–8, before 1904. Vocal scores.

Presented by Henry Festing Jones, Esq.

38188. SONGS AND HARPSICHORD SOLOS; early to mid 18th cent. The composers identified include Arne, W. Babell, Corelli, Gouge, Greene, Handel, Hart, Hasse, Martin, J. Randall.

38189. COLLECTION OF DANCE, THEATRE AND TRADITIONAL TUNES; begun *circ.* 1696 with additions *circ.* 1722, etc. Violin part (with a treble voice-part for H. Purcell's anthem, 'My song shall be alway'). The other composers identified are Bononcini, T. Doggett, H. Holcombe, D. Purcell, Anthony Thomas.

38488A. LIVERPOOL PAPERS. Miscellaneous volume:

ff. 220b–34. Songs, etc., sung at Ranelagh and Vauxhall, by Worgan, S. Howard, Dibdin, etc.; *circ.* 1750–70.

f. 235. John Stanley: hymn, 'Spirit of Mercy'; 18th cent.

ff. 236–239. Johann Stiastny: three duos for violoncello and bass from *XII Pièces* [1810?].

ff. 240–5. John Ella: Vittoria March for pianoforte with 'cello; before 1838.

Presented by the Hon. Henry Berkeley Portman.

1912

38531. ROBERT VALENTINE: twelve sonatas for two oboes, eighteen 'Sonate à due Oboe sù l'aria di tromba', twelve sonatas for oboe and bass; 1719? Score.

38539. JOHN STURT'S LUTEBOOK: lute music by John Sturt (probably the compiler), R. Kindersley, J. Dowland, A. Holborne, D. Bachelor, R. Johnson; *circ.* 1613–16. The reverse end of the volume contains organ parts of services by Tallis, Byrd, Rogers, Child and O. Gibbons.

38540–63. ROBERT LUCAS PEARSALL, of Willsbridge House, in Bitton, co. Glouc., and afterwards of Wartensee Castle, near St. Gall, Switzerland: musical compositions, many in rough draft; 1836–54, etc. Mainly *autograph* but some are in the hand of the composer's daughter, Philippa Swinnerton. As follows:

38540–1. Sacred music including anthems, hymns, motets, fragments of services, 'Te Deum' and adaptations from works by J. Clarke, T. East, Goudimel, H. Isaac, C. Le Jeune, Marcello, Tallis, etc.

38542. Requiem in G minor; 1853–6.

38543. Fair copies of sacred music; 1841–52.

38544–5. Secular music, etc., including canons, glees, madrigals, fragments of opera and oratorio, songs, orchestral marches, piano and organ solos; 19th cent.

38546. Arrangements from works by madrigal composers and others, including J. Bennet, M. East, Lasso, Morley, Himmel, R. J. S. Stevens, interspersed with sketches of anthems, madrigals, songs, etc., by Pearsall; 1835–8.

38547. A similar collection including anthems, madrigals, parts of a mass, and of services; 1838.

38548. 'Musica Gregoriana' or 'Opinions on the origin and progress of ecclesiastical music, communicated in a suite of letters to the Reverend H. T. Ellacombe', vicar of Bitton, co. Glouc.; 1849–50.

38549–50. 'Psalmodia' or 'An Essay on Psalmtunes . . . in the Church of England'; 1842. Vol. II is a Musical Appendix of chorales, etc.

38551. Letters to John Merewether, D.D., Dean of Hereford, on Church Music; 1850.

38552. Rough notes on the history and theory of music.

38553. Rough drafts of vocal works including anthems, glees, and madrigals.

38554. Fair copies of madrigals, etc., by J. Bennet, Dowland, O. Gibbons, Morley, Palestrina, Tallis, H. Purcell, Tye, Weelkes, Wilbye, etc.

38555–9. Fair copies of madrigals, glees, etc., by English and Italian composers including Anerio, J. Bennet, Bishop, Dowland, M. East, Festa, O. Gibbons, Lasso, Marenzio, Morley, H. Purcell, Stevens, Tye, Ward, S. Webbe senior, etc.

38560. Miscellaneous writings including a catalogue of Pearsall's music library (at Wartensee Castle?), poems, etc.

38561–2. Not of musical interest.

38563. 'Cobbett on Music in VI Letters'; 1839. Written by Pearsall in imitation of the style of William Cobbett.

38599, ff. 133–45. COMMONPLACE-BOOK OF THE SHANN FAMILY of Methley, co. York: fourteen songs, etc.; copied by Richard Shanne, 1611.

38622. LIBRETTI, including an English version of 'Der Freischütz' by Logan, 'The Incas or the Peruvian Virgin' by John Thelwall, airs (words only) for 'Harlequin Omai' by John O'Keeffe, 1785, etc.; 18th–19th cent.

38648. HENRY PURCELL: services and (reversing the volume) anthems by H. Aldrich (arranged from Carissimi), P. Humfrey, M. Wise; transcribed by John Alcock, 1734. Score.

38650. MISCELLANEOUS VOLUME:

G. Hector Berlioz: letter to Édouard Silas; Paris, 6 Jan. 1864. *French*. f. 58.

1913

38668. WILLIAM CROFT: Morning and Evening Service in E flat; 1719. Score. *Autograph*.

38783. LYRA VIOL SOLOS: transcripts in staff notation of the 17th-cent. manuscript in tablature in the Henry Watson Music Library, Manchester, including pieces by C. Coleman, Facy, A. Ferrabosco junior, S. Ives, Jenkins, W. Lawes, C. Simpson, W. Young, and lesser-known composers of whom Richard Sumarte appears to have had a share in the arrangement and compilation of the original volume; 1913.
Presented by Sir Edward Ernest Cooper.

38785. FREDERIC CLAY: opera, 'The Bold Recruit'; 19th cent.
Presented by Mrs. Godfrey Pearse.

38789. WILLIAM CHAPPELL: collection of English song-tunes and a few dances; made for his *Popular Music of the Olden Time*, 1855–9.

38794. MISCELLANEOUS VOLUME:

H. George Thomson of Edinburgh: memorandum concerning the publication of three sonatas and three quintets by Beethoven; Jan. 1810. ff. 155, 155b.

1914

38811. WILLIAM YOUNG: eleven sonatas and nineteen dances for viols transcribed from the Uppsala University Library copy of *Sonate a 3, 4, 5 voci con Allemande, Corranti*, Innsbruck, 1653; 1912–13.

39075, f. 156. YEZIDI or Devil-Worshipper's music; late 19th cent. (From the Layard Papers).
Bequeathed by Dame Mary Evelyn Layard.

39166. SACRED MUSIC: Leonardo Leo, 'Miserere' for two choirs with organ bass, Francesco Feo, Litany, with strings; 18th–19th cent.
Presented by William Barclay Squire, Esq.

39168. MISCELLANEOUS VOLUME:

I. Charles Wesley, musician: letter relating to the illness of his brother, Samuel; *circ.* 1787. ff. 65, 65b.

1915

39180. GEORGE FRIDERIC HANDEL: opera, 'Radamisto'; 18th cent.
Presented by William Barclay Squire, Esq.

39255. MISCELLANEOUS VOLUME:

I. Peter Benoit, Belgian composer: note to J. Alphonse Voorhamme; Antwerp, 1899. *Flemish.* f. 90.
Presented by Monsieur Voorhamme.

1916

No music manuscripts in this series were acquired in this year.

1917

39549. JOHN PEARSALL of Woodbridge: music book containing minuets, etc., for harpsichord including two by Bononcini, dances, marches, songs, etc.; begun by John Pearsall in 1726.
Presented by William Barclay Squire, Esq.

39550–7. SOUTHGATE COLLECTION:

> 39550–4. Fancies, In Nomines and Pavans in 5 and 6 parts by Ward, White, Ravenscroft, Cranford, Dering, Coperario, A. Ferrabosco junior and senior, Byrd, Lupo; *circ.* 1640? Parts. Partly in the hand of Sir Nicholas Le Strange of Hunstanton, with collation notes referring to other contemporary copies.
>
> 39555. Lyra viol music, in tablature: modern tracing by Florence G. Attenborough from a 17th-cent. manuscript formerly in the possession of the Rookwoods of Coldham and then of the Gages of Hengrave, co. Suff., including pieces by Jenkins, J. N[evile], Simon Clarke, C. Simpson, 'N.P.', 'N.Y.'; early 20th cent.
>
> 39556. Lyra viol solos in tablature: quasi-facsimile by Ethel C. M. Higgins of the 17th cent. manuscript in the Henry Watson Music Library, Manchester (see 38783 above for contents); 1912.
>
> 39557. Sir John Goss, organist of St. Paul's Cathedral, 1838–72: sketchbook of musical compositions including anthems, glees, and an opera; 1822–67.

Bequeathed by Dr. Thomas Lea Southgate.

39565–7. Incidental music, dances, sonatas, etc., arranged in sets or suites for wind instruments and strings, including pieces by Paisible, Colasse, Tollet, Morgan, H. Purcell, Finger, Corelli, J. Clarke; late 17th cent. Parts (the second treble part is Add. 30839).

Presented by Augustus Hughes-Hughes, Esq.

39568. JOHANN ADOLF HASSE: opera, 'Artaserse'; 18th cent.

Presented by Augustus Hughes-Hughes, Esq.

39569. COLLECTION OF KEYBOARD PIECES: including twenty-nine suites arranged from works by Lully, N. A. Le Bègue, J. C. de Chambonnières, H. Purcell, M. A. Charpentier, Paisible, J. Clarke, Pepusch, F. Forcer, T. Tollet, P. Colasse, etc., with twelve toccatas, by G. Muffat, etc.; *circ.* 1702. Owned by William Babell (name on the binding).

Presented by Ralph Griffin, Esq., F.S.A.

39570. JOHANN CASPAR RÜTTINGER, Hofmusikus and Organist of the Waisenkirche, Hildburghaussen: 'Allgemeines Choral-Buch, geordnet nach der Liederfolge des neuen Hildburghäusischen Gesangbuchs', 274 chorales mainly by Rüttinger, for four voices, in compressed score, with figured bass and interludes for organ; early 19th cent. *German.* Probably *autograph.*

Presented by Ralph Griffin, Esq., F.S.A.

39571. GEORGE FRIDERIC HANDEL: Passion Music of 1716 in abridged form; 19th cent. The words are from Russell Martineau's translation of Brockes's libretto.

Presented by Richard Alexander Streatfeild, Esq.

39572. ANTHEMS: by Henry VIII?, W. Mundy, O. Gibbons, Tallis, Byrd, Tye, Bull, Child, Blow, R. Parsons, Weldon, Stroud, C. King, J. Clarke, Church, Boyce, Aldrich, etc.; transcribed by Richard Guise, 1768. Score.

Presented by Richard Alexander Streatfeild, Esq.

39674. MISCELLANEOUS VOLUME:

H. Bernardo Pasquini: ricercari, copied by J. S. Shedlock from a Berlin manuscript, with a thematic index of the remaining contents of the volume; early 20th cent. ff. 22–44b.

Presented by John South Shedlock, Esq.

   I (1). William Smith Rockstro: letter to Samuel Butler enclosing a puzzle canon; March 1892. ff. 45–8.
      (2). H. F. Jones: counterpoint exercises corrected by Rockstro, with *autograph* canons by Rockstro. ff. 49–55b.

Presented by Henry Festing Jones, Esq.

1918

39679–80. WILLIAM BARCLAY SQUIRE: letters, mainly to him, from Sir George Grove and many other writers relating to articles in *Grove's Dictionary of Music and Musicians* and the *Dictionary of National Biography*; 1878–1909.

Presented by William Barclay Squire, Esq.

39765–6. BARON EMANUELE D'ASTORGA: songs and duets, in score; 18th cent.

Presented by William Barclay Squire, Esq.

39774. GEORGE FRIDERIC HANDEL: 'The Messiah'; mid 18th cent. Score.

Presented by William Barclay Squire, Esq.

1919

39815. VOCAL WORKS, etc.:

   (1). Motets by G. M. Asola, Steffani, G. B. Martini, Posse, and Ignaz von Seyfried; 18th–19th cent. Score. ff. 1–39b.

(2). C. P. E. Bach: chorus from 'Heilig'; early 19th cent. ff. 40–50b.

(3). John Bennet: song adapted by Edward Taylor; 19th cent. f. 51.

(4). G. Curci, T. Traetta: operatic excerpts; early 19th cent. ff. 53–61b, 62–67.

(5). Three piano sonatas; (watermark 1805.) ff. 68–87.

Presented by William Barclay Squire, Esq.

39816. J. F. LAMPE: songs from the operas 'Britannia' (1732) and 'Dione' (1733); copied by John Christopher Smith, 18th cent. Score.

39817. ANTONIO LOTTI: 'Confitebor' for four voices with instruments; 18th cent. Score.

39845. WILHELM FRIEDRICH ERNST BACH: Concerto Buffo; 1st half 19th cent. Full score. *Autograph.*

39861. THEOBALD BOEHM: 'The construction of flutes and their last improvements'; before 1882. *Autograph.*

Presented by the executors of Christopher Welch, Esq.

39864. WILLIAM HENRY HUSK, Librarian to the Sacred Harmonic Society: papers and notes on music; 19th cent.

Transferred from the Department of Printed Books.

39868. JOHN BENNET'S ORGANBOOK: organ part to anthems and services, etc., by Aldrich, Batten, T. Bennet, Blow, Child, Clarke, Croft, O. Gibbons, Greene, Handel, Humfrey, H. Purcell, Tallis, Tudway, etc.; begun by John Bennet, 1724.

39907. ITALIAN CANTATAS: by G. Bononcini, Viviani, F. C. Lanciani, Abbate Filippo Colonnese, G. Pacieri, B. Pasquini, A. Scarlatti, A. Stradella; 17th–18th cent.

39922. MISCELLANEOUS VOLUME:

F. Copies of music by O. Gibbons, Caldara, Hasse; 19th–20th cent. ff. 19–29b.

Presented by William Barclay Squire, Esq.

1920

39929, ff. 54–362 *passim.* REVEREND THOMAS TWINING: correspondence with Dr. Charles Burney; 1773–85.

39936, f. 14. REVEREND THOMAS TWINING: list of 'Twining's Music on sale valued by Wynne'; before 1804.

39957. HARPSICHORD SOLOS transcribed by Dr. Charles Burney at Chester: by John Christopher Smith, Handel, F. Geminiani, Thomas Arne; 1744.

Presented by Augustus Hughes-Hughes, Esq.

40011B. THE FOUNTAINS FRAGMENTS:
(1). Eight strips of vellum lifted from the binding of 40011A (accounts, etc., of Fountains Abbey, co. York) containing fragments of sequences and hymns; 14th cent. ff. 1–8.
(2). Six paper leaves containing parts of mass settings and motets; mid 15th cent. ff. 9–14.

1921

40080. GIROLAMO FRESCOBALDI: 'Fioretti' for harpsichord; early 17th cent.

40081. LEONARDO LEO: harpsichord solos; copied 1751.

40139. HARPSICHORD PIECES: by G. Spencer, Croft, Handel, Pepusch, J. Eccles, F. Mancini, H. Purcell; after 1714.

Presented by Ronald Assheton Coates, Esq.

40166. MISCELLANEOUS VOLUME:
R. Christina Georgina Rossetti: letter to Herbert Bedford, the composer, giving him permission to publish his setting of 'When I am dead my dearest'; 3 March 1890. f. 152.

Presented by Eric George Millar, Esq., D. Litt., F.S.A.

1922

40636. SAMUEL SEBASTIAN WESLEY: sketches of compositions including anthems, hymns, masses, services, songs, organ solos and arrangements of works by other composers; 18th–19th cent.

Presented by William Barclay Squire, Esq.

40657–61. WILLIAM LAWES: music for two to six viols, in parts, together with pieces by Lupo, Chetwoode, T. Holmes, Coperario, N. Guy, Ward, Ford, Ives, A. Ferrabosco junior, Bull, White, and arrangements for viols of madrigals by Monteverdi, Marenzio, Vecchi, Pallavicino; before 1645. Partly *autograph*.

40725, ff. i, ib. CHORAL SETTING of parts of the Mass for three voices, in score; 14th cent. (Flyleaf from the Blythburgh Priory Chartulary.)

40728. EDWARD ALEXANDER MACDOWELL: 'Ländliche Suite f. grosses Orchester', op. 37; *circ.* 1890–1. Full score and a piano duet arrangement. *Autograph*.
Presented by Mrs. Marian MacDowell, the composer's widow.

40730. MISCELLANEOUS VOLUME:

    B. Johannes Brahms: two letters to the Amtsvogt Blume of Winsen-an-der Luhe referring to Joachim and the Schumanns; im Lahnthal, Sept. 1853, Ulm, 16 Aug. 1854. ff. 3–5.

    I. Sir Charles Hubert Hastings Parry: four letters to Kate Cholditch Smith relating to a performance of his 'Judith' and to the Aviator's Hymn, with one draft reply; 20 Nov. 1903–28 Mar. 1918. ff. 49–56b.
Presented by Miss Kate Cholditch Smith.

1923

40881. WILLIAM STERNDALE BENNETT: overture, 'Wald Nymphen', op. 20; 1838. Full score. *Autograph*.

41063. MISCELLANEOUS VOLUME:

    A. Song, 'The Devil's Progress' or 'Huggle Duggle' arranged, with piano accompaniment, from the song printed in T. D'Urfey's *Wit and Mirth: or Pills to Purge Melancholy*, 1699; 19th cent. ff. 1b–3b.
Presented by Augustus Hughes-Hughes, Esq.

    M. Motet, 'O Salutaris Hostia', for two voices with bass, attributed to Giovanni Battista Pergolesi; 1729 (? a forgery). ff. 93–5.

1924

41091–4. PERUGINI COLLECTION. Vocal music composed or collected by Leonardo Perugini, the composer and opera singer. As follows:

41091–2. Vocal solos, duets, trios and quartets with keyboard accompaniment by Perugini; 1835, 1837, n.d. Mostly *autograph*.

41093–4. Vocal music mainly by Italian composers of the 18th and 19th century including Zingarelli, N. Manfroce, Haydn, B. Asiolo mostly collected by Perugini; 18th–19th cent.

Presented by Mark Edward Perugini, Esq.

41138. HEINRICH LUDWIG VETTER: string quintet in F; late 18th cent. Parts, in the hand of Johannes Matthes (?Kammermusikus to Prince Henry of Prussia.)

Presented by Ronald Assheton Coates, Esq.

41156–8. Three-part vocal and instrumental music by Morales, Byrd, A. Ferrabosco senior, Taverner, R. White, Tallis, Victoria, Johnson, Palestrina, Regnart, Vaet, Marenzio, etc.; early 17th cent. From the group of manuscripts associated with the Paston family (see p. 98).

1925

41205. JOHN BARRETT'S COLLECTION: dance tunes, etc., arranged for harpsichord, by English composers of the 17th and early 18th century including H. Purcell and Blow; 1st half 18th cent. Said (f. ii) to be in the hand of John Barrett, Music Master at Christ's Hospital.

Purchased with the aid of a gift from William Barclay Squire, Esq.

41295. MISCELLANEOUS VOLUME:

P. Ludwig van Beethoven: letter to the household of Cajetan Giannatasio del Rio; 1817. ff. 131, 131b.

Presented by Mrs. Florence Julia Street.

1926

41328. SIR FREDERICK ARTHUR GORE OUSELEY: parts of Morning and Evening Services in C; 19th cent. *Autograph*.

Presented by W. J. Letts, Esq.

41340. MISCELLANEOUS VOLUME:

E. Charles Camille Saint-Saëns: letter to Francis Hueffer, music critic; 27 May 1886. *French*. f. 65.

Presented by F. M. Wood, Esq.

1927

41487. CHARLES CAMILLE SAINT-SAËNS: song, 'Angélus', for tenor and piano; 1918. *Autograph.*

41498, f. 38. LUTE SETTING of the tune, 'Watkin's Ale'; late 16th cent. On a flyleaf at the end of a 16th-cent. copy of Sir Philip Sidney's 'Arcadia'.

41508–10. BUNTING COLLECTION. Irish airs transcribed for piano by Edward Bunting (the bulk of Bunting's collection is in the library of Queen's University, Belfast). As follows:

> 41508. Bunting's copies of his *A General Collection of the Ancient Music of Ireland*, [1809], and his *New Edition of a General Collection of the Ancient Irish Music*, n.d., with *autograph* corrections and annotations; early 19th cent.

> 41509. Collection of airs mainly published in his third collection, *The Ancient Music of Ireland*, 1840; *circ.* 1825–40. *Autograph.*

> 41510. 'Selections chiefly from original Irish Poetry intended for the Musical publication of E. Bunting': lyrics published in the 1809 volume; 1808–9. With *autograph* notes.

41567. MISCELLANEOUS VOLUME:

> D. Song, 'Shepherd of the Hills', as dictated over the telephone from New York by 'Horatio Nicholls' (pseudonym of Lawrence Wright) and noted down in London by Jack Hylton. f. 73.

Presented by the composer.

> R. Ambroise Thomas: letter on money matters; 15 Feb. 1847. *French.* ff. 264, 264b.

1928

41570–4. EDWARDS PAPERS. Papers and letters addressed to Frederick George Edwards, F.R.A.M., editor of *The Musical Times*; 1897–1909. As follows:

> 41570. Letters of Mendelssohn, Sullivan, Sir J. Stainer, Stanford, Parry, Coleridge-Taylor, Elgar and *autograph* musical fragments; 19th–20th cent.

> 41571. Felix Mendelssohn Bartholdy: motet, 'Lauda Sion'; 1846–7. Vocal score.

> 41572. Elizabeth Mounsey: letters relating to Mendelssohn with two from her sister, Ann S. Bartholomew, widow of William Bartholomew etc.; 1889–1903.

41573. Letters of Marie Benecke, daughter of Mendelssohn, and other members of her family; 1885–98.

41574. Miscellaneous letters, chiefly from musicians; 1835–1909.

41628–35. PERABO COLLECTION. Musical manuscripts collected by Johann Ernst Perabo, pianist (d. 1920). Mostly *autograph*. As follows:

41628. Letters of musicians including Beethoven, Brahms, Czerny, Liszt, Mendelssohn, Leopold Mozart, W. A. Mozart, Robert and Clara Schumann, Weber; 1783–1910.

41629.
> (1). J. S. Bach: first oboe part of Cantata no. 130, 'Herr Gott dich loben alle wir'; contemporary *copy*.
> (2). Franz Schubert: fragment of 'Die Sehnsucht', op. 39; 1819. *Autograph*.
> (3). Robert Schumann: overture to 'Genoveva', op. 81, arranged for piano; 1850. *Printed* with *autograph* note.

41630.
> (1). Ludwig van Beethoven: piano part of the Triple Concerto, op. 56; *circ.* 1807. Contemporary *copy* as sent to the printer with *autograph* corrections.
> (2). Franz Schubert: two songs, 'Der Fischer', op. 5, no. 3, 'Wandrers Nachtlied', op. 4, no. 3, and Three Italian Songs, op. 83; 1815, 1827. *Autograph*.

41631. Ludwig van Beethoven: *Drei Sonaten fürs Klavier dem Hochwürdigsten Erzbischofe und Kurfürsten zu Köln Maximilian Friedrich ... gewidmet* [WoO 47], 1783. *Printed* with *autograph* annotations.

41632. Franz Schubert: Mass in B flat, op. 141; 1815. *Autograph*.

41633. Johann Ernst Eberlin and Johann Michael Haydn: masses, motets and church music mostly in the hand of Leopold Mozart; before 1774.

41634.
> (1). J. M. Haydn: Messa da Requiem in B flat; *circ.* 1806. *Autograph. Imperfect.*
> (2). Carl Maria von Weber: six variations for pianoforte, with accompaniment for violin and 'cello, on 'Woher mag das wohl kommen' by Abbé Vogler; 1804. *Autograph*.

41635. Robert Franz: arrangements for alto and tenor, with piano accompaniment, of works by Bach; 1859. Partly *autograph*.

Presented by Edward Perry Warren, Esq., pupil of J. E. Perabo.

41636–9. HIPKINS PAPERS: correspondence of Alfred Hipkins, F.S.A., and other members of his family, mainly relating to ancient musical instruments, pitch, etc.; 1895–1927.

Presented by Miss Edith J. Hipkins, daughter of Alfred Hipkins.

41642. CHARLES VILLIERS STANFORD: 'The Revenge', op. 24, setting of Tennyson's poem for chorus and orchestra; 1886. Full score. *Autograph.*

41667. MISCELLANEOUS VOLUME:
I. The MacVeagh Fragment: two vellum leaves containing five incomplete motets and one ballad; 14th cent. ff. 26–27 b.

1929

41671. HENRY FESTING JONES: comic opera, 'The Crystal Casket'; early 20th cent. Piano score. *Autograph.*

Presented by A. T. Bartholomew, Esq.

41677. HENRY FESTING JONES: songs with piano accompaniment; 19th–20th cent. *Autograph.*

Presented by A. T. Bartholomew, Esq.

41771–9. SIR GEORGE SMART, musician and conductor: correspondence, papers, etc.; 19th cent. As follows:

41771. Correspondence mainly relating to the Philharmonic Society; 1790–1867.

41772. 'Events in the life of George T. Smart'; 1776–1861.

41773–4. Journals of tours to France and Germany; 1802, 1825.

41775. Theatrical bills of performances attended by Smart on his tour of Germany; Brussels, 2 August–Paris, 1 December 1825.

41776. Tour to Bonn to attend the unveiling of Beethoven's statue; 1845.

41777. Correspondence and papers relating to royal concerts and ceremonials and the annual Festival of the Sons of the Clergy; 1819–66.

41778. Papers relating to Weber's last visit to England and death at Smart's house; 1826.

41779. 'The Philharmonic Society: Lists of the Subscribers, Members and Associates, with remarks on the Concerts, etc. . . . by George T. Smart'; 1813–60.

Presented by Hugh Bertram Cox, Esq., C.B.

41847. JOHN WELDON: three verse anthems; early 18th cent. *Autograph.*
Presented by Ralph Griffin, Esq., F.S.A.

14866. JOHANNES BRAHMS: Rhapsody in E flat, op. 119, no. 4; 1893. *Autograph.*

1930

42050. ANTONÍN DVOŘÁK: violoncello concerto in A major, with piano accompaniment; 1865. Score. *Autograph.*

42064. JACQUES OFFENBACH: comic opera, 'Fantasio'; 1872. Full score. Mainly *autograph.*

42065. VAUGHAN RICHARDSON: four verse anthems; early 18th cent. *Autograph?*
Presented by Ralph Griffin, Esq., F.S.A.

42110–11. CHARLES KENSINGTON SALAMAN: songs, with piano accompaniment; 1836–94. Mostly copied by Elizabeth Windsor.
Presented by Harold Reeves, Esq.

42112. ELIZABETH WINDSOR: songs; 1836–9. Mostly *autograph.*
Presented by Harold Reeves, Esq.

42181. MISCELLANEOUS VOLUME:
D. Juan de Arriaga: piano arrangement of airs from the opera, 'Los esclavos felices', 1820; copied in 1930. ff. 13–14b.
Presented by José de Arriaga, Esq.

1931

42225. SIR GEORGE SMART: memoranda book; 1793–1863.
Presented by Hugh Bertram Cox, Esq., C.B.

42233. EDWARD SPEYER: letters to him from Grove, Hadow, Henschel, Parry, Stanford, A. G. Thomas, H. Wood; 1876–1930. With *autograph* music by Charles Horsley, 1841 (ff. 301b–302) and Hermann T. Petschke, 1841 (f. 302b).
Presented by Edward Speyer, Esq.

42501. CHARLES KENSINGTON SALAMAN: songs; 1836–8. Partly *autograph* and partly in the hand of Elizabeth Windsor.
Presented by Harold Reeves, Esq.

1932

42718. JOSEPH JOACHIM: letters to his parents and brother; 1844–81. *German.*
Presented by Miss Agnes E. Keep.

43377. MISCELLANEOUS VOLUME:

    A. Jenny Lind: fragment of a letter relating to a professional engagement; n.d. ff. 1, 1b.

Presented by Sir Charles Reed Peers, C.B.E.

    E. Michael William Balfe: letter to Léon Carvalho, stage director, relating to the Paris production of 'The Bohemian Girl'; 18 April 1868. ff. 15–16.

Presented by Arthur Watson, Esq.

    O. Programme of a concert on RMS. 'Teutonic' *signed* by Paderewski, etc.; 1896. ff. 96, 96b.

Presented by John Richard England, Esq.

1933

43468. CARL MARIA VON WEBER: selection from the opera, 'Der Freischütz', made by Louis Antoine Jullien; 1852. Full score. Possibly the *autograph* of Jullien.

43469–70. H. S. A. VOGELS: musical compositions. Probably *autograph.*

    43469. L'Angélus', op. 1, 'Fantasie', op. 19, both for viola and orchestra; 1850, n.d. Full scores.

    43470. 'Le Chant de la Berceuse', op. 41, for violin with piano and 'cello accompaniment; 1863.

1934

43736. GUILLAUME DUFAY: motets, songs, etc., transcribed by J. F. R. Stainer; 1895–8.
Presented by John Frederick Randall Stainer, Esq.

43796. JUAN DE ARRIAGA Y BALZOLA: overture in F minor; after 1818.
Presented by José de Arriaga.

1935

43863. MAURICE GREENE: six verse anthems; copied by John Barker, 1725.
Presented by Thomas Adams, Esq.

43867. LADISLAS JOSEPH PHILIP PAUL ZAVERTAL: chorus, mazurka, four songs, and hymn arrangement, together with an *autograph* song of his father, Vaclav Hugo Zavertal; 1872–83. *Autograph.*

Presented by Dr. Henry George Farmer.

43902, ff. 156–7. FRANÇOIS DELSARTE: song, 'Toi dont l'amour'; [*circ.* 1868].

Presented by Miss Gertrude Mary Tuckwell, C.H.

43970. GIOACCHINO ANTONIO ROSSINI: 'Stabat Mater'; 1841? Full score. *Autograph.*

Presented by Julian George Lousada, Esq. in memory of Christine Nilsson.

1936

44880. JAMES HAMILTON CLARKE: string quartet in A major, op. 246; 1884. Score. *Autograph.*

Presented by Richard Ridgill Trout, Esq.

44919. MISCELLANEOUS VOLUME:

S. John Cheshire: 'Remembrance' for harp; 1900. *Autograph.* ff.89–92.

Presented by Miss Zoë Cheshire, daughter of the composer.

HH. James Hamilton Siree Clarke: list of manuscript works; 20th cent. *Typewritten.* ff. 171–4.

Presented by Richard Ridgill Trout, Esq.

1937

44940. FRANZ JOSEPH HAYDN: arrangements for two pianos and flute of the London Symphonies in E flat, G, B flat and D (nos. 99, 100, 102, 104); late 18th–19th cent.

45102. MISCELLANEOUS VOLUME:

A, Q. Music by the Zavertal family:

A. Ladislas Joseph Zavertal: song, 'If 'tis love to wish you near'; 1885. *Autograph* title-page. ff. 1–4.

Q. Vaclav Hugo Zavertal: 'God Save the King', arranged for military band, with notes on brass instruments; before 1899. *Autograph* ff. 93, 93 b.

Presented by Dr. Henry George Farmer.

E. Gioacchino Antonio Rossini:

(1). Certificate relating to his choice of Mme Dotti to sing in his 'Stabat Mater' at Pesaro, 1859; Paris, 28 May 1861. *French. Signed.* f. 18.

(2). Song, 'Conçois tu toutes mes douleurs'; n.d. *Autograph.* ff. 19–20b.

P. George Frideric Handel: trio for two clarinets and corno di caccia; copied by John Parr, bassoonist of Sheffield, from Fitzwilliam Museum MS. 264, 1934. ff. 83–91.

Presented by John Parr, Esq.

Y. Samuel Wesley: letter to John Thomas Smith; n.d. ff. 137–138b.

Presented by Wilmarth Sheldon Lewis, Esq.

1938

45183. CARL PHILIPP EMANUEL BACH: trio in G for flute, violin and (figured) bass; 18th cent. Parts.

Presented by the Worcestershire Association of Music Societies.

45206, f. 31b. THREE DANCE TUNES (treble part only) including 'Welcome to bichborow [Beachborough]', with a list of 'The Childrens Dauncis', including 'The new spannilettoe', 'The new sahoe', 'The Durettoe', etc.; early 17th cent. (In a volume of the Brockman Papers.)

Presented by members of the Brockman family, through Miss Phyllis Brockman.

45224. MISCELLANEOUS VOLUME:

B. Sir Edward German: four letters to Robert Furber; 1901, n.d. ff. 3–11b.

Presented by Miss Jessie Rendle Furber.

Q. Jenny Lind: fragments of a letter to ——; after 1851. ff. 79–80.

Transferred from the Department of Prints and Drawings.

1939

45498. MISCELLANEOUS VOLUME:

Q. Samuel Sebastian Wesley: four letters to Rev. W. E. Dickson, Precentor of Ely Cathedral; 1860–62. ff. 99–110.

Presented by Capt. Arthur J. Lord, D.S.O.

1940

45580, ff. 1–32b. RICHARD BLECHYNDEN: naval songs (words only) collected by; 1781.

Bequeathed by Richard Blechynden, Esq., great-grandson of the compiler.

1941

45850. MISCELLANEOUS VOLUME:

B. Sir Charles Villiers Stanford:

(1). 'Ulster', setting of a poem by William Wallace; 1913. *Autograph*. ff. 2, 2b.

(2). 'An Ulster March-tune', arranged for orchestra; n.d. Condensed score. *Autograph*. ff. 3, 3b.

(3). March for orchestra; n.d. Condensed score. *Autograph*. ff. 3b–4.

Presented by Cecil Forsyth, Esq.

M.   Cipher message in the form of a song allegedly sent by a loyalist lady (?Jane Lane, afterwards Lady Clement Fisher) to Charles II at Boscobel; copied by Ellen Lane, early 19th cent. f. 68.

Presented by Gerald Lawrence, Esq.

1942

No music manuscripts in this series were acquired in this year.

1943

45882. ALESSANDRO STRADELLA: 'Oratorio di S. Giovanni Battista'; late 17th cent. Score.

Presented by Edward Wyndham Hulme, Esq.

45898. WILLIAM HENRY LIDDLE: cantata, 'Horsa'; *circ.* 1889. Score.

Transferred from the Department of Printed Books.

1944

45909. SIR WILLIAM STERNDALE BENNETT: Preludium in B flat for pianoforte; 1863. *Autograph*.

Presented by Sidney Joseph Madge, Esq., F.S.A.

45934–50. ETHEL SMYTH COLLECTION. Musical compositions of Dame Ethel Smyth. Mostly *autograph*. As follows:

45934–7.   'Fantasio', comic opera; 1892–4. Full score.

45938.   'Der Wald', opera; 1899–1901. Full score.

45939–41. 'Les Naufrageurs', opera; 1903–4. Full score.

45942–3. 'The Boatswain's Mate', comic opera; 1913–14. Condensed score.

45944.   Songs of Sunrise, nos. 2, 3; 1911. Score (of no. 2 only) and band parts.

45945.   Songs of the Sea; 1913.

45946.   Variations on 'Bonny Sweet Robin'; 1927.

45947.   Organ Prelude on a traditional Irish Air; 1938.

45948.   Concerto for violin, horn and orchestra arranged by the composer as a trio for violin, horn (or viola or 'cello) and piano; 1927.

45949.   Sonata in C minor for 'cello and piano, op. 5; 1887.

45950.   Sonata in A minor for violin and piano, op. 7; 1887.

Presented by Brigadier-General Robert Napier Smyth, C.B.E., D.S.O., brother of the composer.

1945

45984. IGNAZ MOSCHELES: 'Grande Sonate Symphonique à Quatre Mains, op. 112; 1845. *Autograph.*

Presented by Herbert C. Percy, Esq.

46122. TENOR PARTS OF THE ORATORIOS, 'The Messiah' and 'Judas Maccabeus' by Handel, and 'Judith' and 'Abel' by Arne; after 1761.

Presented by Lieutenant Philip Christopher Roscoe, R.N.V.R.

46134–5. VERNON MANUSCRIPTS: music manuscripts from the collection of George Warren (d. 1866), 5th Baron Vernon; 19th cent. As follows:

46134A, B. Sicilian canzone.

46135. Miscellaneous vocal and instrumental music including stornelli by A. Schimon, Neapolitan canzone, tarantellas, songs by F. W. Kücken, waltzes (spurious) attributed to Beethoven, and an anonymous piano duet in F.

Presented by the heirs of George Warren, 5th Baron Vernon, with a collection of printed music.

46172. MISCELLANEOUS VOLUME:

H. Franz Joseph Haydn: divertimento in E flat for horn, violin and 'cello [Hoboken, IV. 5*]; transcribed by E. Mandyczewski before 1934. ff. 50–1b.

Presented by Walter Fielding Holloway Blandford, Esq.

1946

46347. FELIX MENDELSSOHN BARTHOLDY: 'Hear my prayer', arrangement for soprano solo, chorus and orchestra; *circ.* 1847.

Bequeathed by the Rev. Stanford Frederick Hudson Robinson.

46362. MISCELLANEOUS VOLUME:

H. G. J. Learmont Drysdale: aria from the opera, 'Fionn and Tera'; 1908. *Autograph.*

Presented by Miss Janey Drysdale.

1947

46378B, f. 3. Angelo Notari: letter to Dr. Samuel Bave; 1642.

46396. Compositions or arrangements for the horn, with accompaniments for strings, etc., mostly owned by or associated with Giovanni Puzzi (d. 1876) and including probable *autographs* of Francesco Schira and Louis Emmanuel Jadin; mid 19th century. Scores and parts.

Presented by Walter Fielding Holloway Blandford, Esq.

46452, f.iv. Setting of Psalm cxi; late 16th cent. Fragments of one voice-part. *Latin.*

From the binding of a volume presented by Sir Charles Scott Sherrington, O.M.

1948

46839. MISCELLANEOUS VOLUME:

C. Vellum fragment with musical notation formerly used as a seal tag; 13th cent. *French.*

L. Anton Schindler: letter to Charles Neate referring to negotiations for the sale of the former's collection of Beethoven manuscripts; 6 August 1845. *German.*

Presented by Heinrich Eisemann, Esq.

1949

46843. GIOVANNI BOTTESINI: Duetto for violin and double bass with orchestra; 19th cent. Score.

Presented by Henry Samuel Sterling, Esq., Hon. R.A.M.

46857–63. DAME ETHEL SMYTH: early works and sketches. Mostly *autograph*. As follows:

46857. Early works, exercises and sketches for the piano, including three sonatas, variations, two preludes and fugues; *circ.* 1877–82.

46858–9. Five early string quartets; *circ.* 1878–84. Scores, with some parts.

46860. Early works for strings, etc., including the 'Hildebrand Quartet', Introduction and Fugue in B minor, preludes and fugues for organ; *circ.* 1880–1913.

46861. Early vocal works including sacred part-songs, rounds, songs, op. 3, 4, with *copies* of two songs, 'Edward' and 'Botschaft' by Brahms; *circ.* 1876–86.

46862. Song of Love, op. 8, for soprano, tenor, chorus and orchestra; *circ.* 1880–4.

46863. Miscellaneous sketches and fragments; 1888–1930.

Presented in the name of the late Mrs. Lincoln Cary Elwes, niece of the composer.

46912. MISCELLANEOUS VOLUME:
N. Sir Alexander Mackenzie: letter to F. Dolmer; 26 Jan. 1901.

Presented by Herbert E. Friend, Esq.

1950

47215. VASLAV NIJINSKY: choreographic score of the ballet to Debussy's 'L'Après-midi d'un Faune'; Budapest, August–September 1915. *Autograph.*

Presented by Mme Romola Nijinsky, widow of Vaslav Nijinsky.

47216. AUGUSTUS HUGHES-HUGHES: letters addressed to him on musical subjects from musical scholars, including C. van den Borren, W. Chappell, W. H. Cummings, F. Kidson, W. Westley Manning, Count G. de Saint Foix, S. Royle Shore, Dr. T. L. Southgate; 1883–1922.

Presented by Augustus Hughes-Hughes, Esq.

47219. LADISLAS ZAVERTAL: Sinfonia to his opera, 'Luisa Strozzi' or 'Una Notte a Firenze'; circ. 1875. Full score. *Autograph.*

Presented by Miss Mirra Caro Elsa Zavertal.

47220. BARON BODOG ORCZY: opera, 'Sisyphus'; 2 March 1884. Full score. *Autograph.* With a *printed* libretto by Frederick and H. L. Corder.

Presented by Mrs. Eleanor Clementina Corder.

47446. COLLECTION OF SONG AND DANCE TUNES (mainly treble part only) by Handel, Babell, J. Bannister, J. Eccles, J. Barrett, H. Purcell, Monsieur de Moivre, Monsieur Latour, Pepusch, Corelli, Dr. Morgan, J. Clarke, Geminiani, Dieupart, Bononcini, Greene and anonymous; mostly copied by William Pitt, circ. 1722, with subsequent additions.

Presented by G. D. Hornblower, Esq.

1951

47602. HECTOR BERLIOZ: letters to T. Ritter, etc.; 1848–60. *French.*

Presented by Albert William Ganz, Esq.

1952

47683. DRAWINGS AND DESCRIPTIONS OF MUSICAL INSTRUMENTS referred to in the Old Testament; 11th cent. One leaf (formerly Holkham MS 750).

47688. JOHN PRATT WOOLER: libretto of the operetta, 'The Ring and the Keeper', set by W. H. Montgomery; circ. 1859.

47775. CANON K. H. MACDERMOTT: 'The Old Church Gallery Minstrels', notes and extracts on church bands and singers of the 16th–19th century in scrap-book form; 20th cent.

Presented by the compiler.

47776–7. ITALIAN ARIETTE, mostly anonymous, but including single items attributed to S. Mayr, F. Paer, G. Niccolini, V. Trento, two to M. Portogallo, and a number (in 47777) to M. Bevilacqua; after 1802.

Presented by C. F. Simkins, Esq.

47804–38. GUSTAV THEODORE HOLST: musical compositions, mainly unpublished; 1887–1934. *Autograph.* As follows:

47804. 'Horatius' for voices and orchestra; 1887. Full score.

47805. 'Lansdown Castle', operetta; 1892. Vocal score.

47806. 'The Revoke', opera; 1895. Full score.

47807. 'The Magic Mirror', opera; 1896. Sketches, with other miscellaneous sketches.

47808. Early songs, 1896, 1902, etc.: 'Awake my Heart', 'My Joy', beg. 'My Spirit sang all Day', 'Soft and gently', Invocation to Dawn, beg. 'Light hath come', 'Fain would I change that Note', 'Calm is the Morn', 'In a Wood', 'I will not let thee go', 'My true Love hath my Heart', 'Lovely kind and kindly loving', Cradle Song, beg. 'Sweet Dreams', 'Peace'.

47809. Early part-songs: 'Fair is the World', n.d.; 'Her Eyes the Glow-worm lend thee', [1902].

47810. 'Clear and cool', for five-part chorus and orchestra; n.d. [1897]. Full score.

47811. 'Winter Idyll', for orchestra; 1897. Full score.

47812. 'Ornulf's Drapa', for baritone and orchestra; Jan. 1900. Full score.

47813. 'Walt Whitman', overture; 1899. Full score.

47814. Cotswolds Symphony; completed 24 July 1900. Full score.

47815. 'The Youth's Choice', musical idyll in one act; n.d. [1902]. Full score.

47816. 'Indra', symphonic poem, op. 13; 3 April 1903. Full score.

47817. 'The Mystic Trumpeter', scena for soprano and orchestra, op. 18; n.d. [1904]. Full score.

47818. 'A Song of the Night', for violin and orchestra, op. 19, no. 1; n.d. [1905]. Full score.

47819. 'Invocation', for 'cello and small orchestra, op. 19, no. 2; n.d. [1911]. Full score.

47820. Songs of the West, for wind band; n.d. Full score.

47821-3. 'Sita', opera; [1899-1906]. Full score.

47824. Suite in E flat, for military band; [1909]. Full score.

47825. Second Suite in F, for military band; n.d. [1911]. Full score.

47826. 'Phantastes', suite for orchestra, op. 29, no. 2; [1911].

47827. 'Phantastes', string quartet, op. 36; n.d.

47828. 'Sneezing Charm'; n.d. Full score.

47829. 'The Lure', ballet; n.d. [1921]. Full score.

47830. Sketch of the First Choral Symphony; n.d. [1923-4].

47831. Second Choral Symphony; *circ.* 1931. Fragments.

47832. Moorside Suite, for brass band; n.d. [1928]. Full score.

47833. 'Mr Shilkret's Maggot', for jazz band; n.d. Full score.

47834. Late fragments including: 'When the Dawn', 'How beautiful are thy Feet', Gavotte, trio and jigg.

47835. Unfinished symphony; n.d. A few sketches.

47836. Notebook containing musical sketches; 1928.

47837. Notebook containing musical sketches; 1929.

47838. Notebook containing musical sketches; 1933-4.

Presented by Mrs. Isobel and Miss Imogen Holst, widow and daughter of the composer.

47839. J. S. BACH: choruses in the St. Matthew Passion said to have been used for the performance under Mendelssohn in Berlin, 11 March 1829. Eight vocal part-books. *German copies.*

Presented by Messrs. Novello & Co., Ltd.

47841. MISCELLANEOUS VOLUME:

H. Johannes Brahms: letter to ——; Vienna, n.d.

1953

47843-62. THE MEYERSTEIN BEQUEST. Music manuscripts collected by E. H. W. Meyerstein; late 16th cent.–20th cent. Partly *autograph.* As follows:

47843. Letters and papers of musicians including C. P. E. Bach, Berlioz, Clementi, Grétry, E. T. A. Hoffman, Hummel, Mendelssohn, Constanza von Nissen, Weber; 18th–19th cent.

47844. Counter-tenor part-book containing Latin motets by Byrd, Lasso, Parsons, Shepherd, Strogers, Taverner, Tye, R. White; after 1581.

47845. Anthems by Blow, Humfrey, H. Purcell, Turner, Tucker, Byrd, with a few canons by 'W. G.' [William Gregory?] Locke, C. Gibbons; 17th–18th cent.

47846. Keyboard music mainly anonymous but including items by J. Clarke, John? Barrett and Lord Byron, together with two songs by J. Weldon and J. Eccles; late 17th or early 18th cent.

47847. French songs, mainly anonymous but including one item by Jean Jacques Rousseau; late 18th cent.

47848. George Frideric Handel: opera, 'Amadigi di Gaula'; copied by John Christopher Smith, *circ.* 1715. Full score.

47849. Franz Joseph Haydn: Symphony in F, no. 40; 1763. Full score. *Autograph.*

47850. Wolfgang Amadeus Mozart: concerto in E flat, K. 271, for piano, 2 violins, 2 oboes, 2 horns, viola and bass; late 18th cent. Parts.

47851. Ludwig van Beethoven: violin concerto, op. 61 (and piano version); 1808. Full score. *Copy* with *autograph* annotations.

47852. Ludwig van Beethoven: 'Lied aus der Ferne', WoO 137, and sketches for 'Der Liebende', WoO 139, with a sketch for op. 59, no. 1?; *circ.* 1809, etc. Full score. *Autograph.*

47853. Carl Maria von Weber: 'Grand Concert pour le Piano-forte', published as op. 11; 1810. Full score. *Autograph.*

47854. Album including a cadenza by Clementi and an unidentified piano sonata; late 18th–early 19th cent.

47855. John Field: piano parts only of concertos nos. 1–5 and piano quintet; 1818, *circ.* 1820 (no. 5). *Printed* copies with *autograph* corrections.

47856. Johann Nepomuk Hummel: duet, 'Lass uns in Trauer scheiden' from 'Jeannot und Colin', op. 72; 24 studies for piano, op. 125; Grand Rondo Brillante for piano with flute or violin, op. 126; early 19th cent., *circ.* 1833, *circ.* 1835. Partly *autograph.*

47857. Johann Baptist Cramer: Seize Nouvelles Études for piano, op. 81; 1835. *Autograph.*

47858. Felix Mendelssohn Bartholdy: piano quartets in C minor and F minor, opp. 1, 2; after 1823. Scores.

47859A, B. Felix Mendelssohn Bartholdy: letters, draft translations (by William Bartholomew) and music relating to the first performance of 'Elijah' at the Birmingham Festival, 1846, and its subsequent revision and publication; 1846–52. Mostly in the hand of William Bartholomew but including eleven *autograph* letters of Mendelssohn.

47860. Miscellaneous:

    (1). William Boyce: 'Macbeth'; 18th cent. *copy* of the string parts for his edition, *The Original Songs Airs and Chorusses ... in ... Macbeth ... by Matthew Locke,* [*circ.* 1770]. Most of the music is now attributed to Richard Leveridge.

    (2). Muzio Clementi: 'Canone Finito, a 3' for 2 violins and viola; 1821. *Autograph.*

    (3). Claude Debussy: fragment from the uncompleted opera, 'La Chute de la Maison Usher'; early 20th cent. *Autograph.*

    (4). Giuseppe Jozzi: Allegro Moderato in C for keyboard; 18th cent.

    (5). Étienne Henri Méhul: fragment in full score from 'Horatius Coclès'?; late 18th cent. *Autograph.*

    (6). Felix Mendelssohn Bartholdy: Variations Sérieuses for piano, op. 54; 1841. *Autograph.*

47861A. Miscellaneous *autograph* music:

(1). Frédéric Chopin: sketch for the mazurka in C, op. 56, no. 2; 1843.

(2). Heinrich August Marschner: song, 'Zuruf'; 1853.

(3). Wolfgang Amadeus Mozart: (i) fragment containing on the recto the cadenza K. 624 (626a), and on the verso part of a Minuet in F (an early draft for K. 168?); *circ.* 1773;-(ii) fragment (bar 65 to the end) of the first movement of the piano sonata in B flat, K. 570; 1789.

(4). Album leaf containing a piano piece by J. P. J. Rode and a canon by E. T. A. Hoffman; 1820.

(5). Franz Schubert: (i) 'Morgenlied' and 'Abendlied'; 1815;-(ii) Sketches for his 'Stabat Mater' (in Klopstock's German translation); 1816;- (iii) 'Vater! schenk mir diese Stunde'; 1820.

(6). Louis Spohr: fragment of the finale of the second piano trio, op. 123; 1842.

(7). Abbé Maximilian Stadler: Fugue in C for piano; early 19th cent.

(8). Carl Maria von Weber: songs (i) 'Zur Freude ward gebohren'; 1812;- (ii) 'From Chindara's warbling fount'; 1826.

47861B. Carl Maria von Weber: piano score of the last section of 'Der erste Ton'; 1810. *Autograph.*

47862. Miscellaneous music transcribed by E. H. W. Meyerstein from early printed editions of Field, Weber, Clementi and S. Paxton; 20th cent.

Bequeathed by Edward Harry William Meyerstein, Esq.

47894. FRANZ ANTON ROSETTI: concerto for bassoon and orchestra; 18th cent. Parts.

47895. RICHARD ALEXANDER STREATFEILD: 'The Pilgrim's Progress', libretto (based on Bunyan) of a symphonic drama for which it was intended that Elgar should write the music, with a prologue in the hand of Elgar; 20th cent. *Typewritten.*

47898. SIR WILLIAM WALTON: 'Te Deum' composed for the coronation of Queen Elizabeth II; 1952–3. Full score. *Autograph.*

Presented by the composer.

47900–8. SIR EDWARD ELGAR: *autograph* sketches of musical works; 19th– 20th cent. As follows:

47900A. Sketches for 'Bizarrerie', op. 13, no. 2; Vesper Voluntaries, op. 14; 'La Capricieuse', op. 17; 'O Happy Eyes', op. 18, no. 1; 'Froissart', op. 19; Serenade for Strings, op. 20; Spanish Serenade, op. 23; 'The Black Knight', op. 25; 'The Snow' and 'Fly Singing Bird', op. 26, nos. 1 and 2; 'From the Bavarian Highlands', op. 27; 'The Light of Life', op. 29.

47900B. *Printed* copies of op. 25, op. 26, nos. 1 and 2, op. 29.

47901A. 'The Banner of St. George', op. 33; 'Caractacus', op. 35.

47901B. *Printed* copy of op. 35.

47902. 'Sea Pictures', op. 37; 'The Dream of Gerontius', op. 38.

47903. 'Pomp and Circumstance', op. 39, nos. 1–3, 5; 'In the Dawn' and 'Speak Music', op. 41, nos. 1 and 2; 'Grania and Diarmid' (Funeral March), op. 42; 'Dream Children', op. 43, nos. 1 and 2; Coronation Ode, op. 44; Five part-songs from the Greek Anthology, op. 45, nos. 2, 3, 4; Introduction and Allegro, op. 47.

47904A, B. 'The Apostles', op. 49: music and libretto.

47905A, B. 'The Kingdom', op. 51: music and libretto.

47906. A few musical sketches and drafts of the libretto for Elgar's projected Third Oratorio.

47907A. 'There is sweet Music', 'O wild west Wind' and 'Owls', op. 53, nos. 1, 3, 4; 'The Reveille', op. 54; Symphony in A flat, op. 55; 'The River', op. 60, no. 2; Coronation Offertorium, op. 64; Coronation March, op. 65; 'Great is the Lord', op. 67.

47907B. 'Falstaff', op. 68.

47908. 'The Music Makers', op. 69; 'Give unto the Lord', op. 74; 'The Spirit of England', op. 80, nos. 1–3; 'Dry those fair, those crystal Eyes', no. 19; 'Skizze für Klavier', no. 27; 'Fear not O Land', no. 43; 'So many true Princesses', no. 63; Sonatina, no. 64; 'The Rapid Stream', no. 67; 'When Swallows Fly', no. 68; 'Mina', no. 70; 'The Woodland Stream', no. 71; Orchestration of the Funeral March from Chopin's B flat minor Sonata.

Presented by Mrs. Carice Elgar Blake, daughter of the composer.

48212. MISCELLANEOUS VOLUME:

O. Piano music by Clementi, Durante, Cramer, anonymous waltzes and duets; early 19th cent.

Presented by Cecil Hopkinson, Esq.

1954

48302. SAMUEL WESLEY: Trio in F for two flutes and piano; 1836. Score. *Autograph.*

Presented by John Parr, Esq.

48303. PETER WARLOCK: 'Cod-pieces', suite for piano, op. 1, written under the pseudonym, 'Prosdocimus de Beldamandis, junior'; 20th cent. *Autograph.*

Presented by William Augustus Henry King, Esq.

48304–11. LOEWENBERG COLLECTION. Notebooks, etc., relating to the history of opera compiled by Dr. Alfred Loewenberg (1902–49) supplementing information in the *Annals of Opera, 1597–1940*, 1943. As follows:

48304. Lists of operas.

48305–7. Opera in various countries.

48308–9. Notes on various subjects related to opera.

48310. Libretti, librettists, translators.

48311. Bibliography of opera.

Presented by Mrs. Edith Loewenberg, widow of the compiler.

48345. Dr. Charles Burney: fragments of his memoirs and part of a common-place-book (including a few fragments for his history of music); 1742–50, 1755–60.

48346–8. ITALIAN VOCAL MUSIC:

48346. Arias, duets, etc., by Palmela, Farinelli, Paisiello, Sarti, Blanquin, Porpora, Pergolesi?, Rossini, etc.; early 19th cent.

48347. Arias, duets, etc., including items by L. Moretti, Trento, Sarti, G. Millico, Leo, Paer, etc., Marche religieuse by L. van Esch; mainly early 19th cent.

48348. Venetian canzonette, notturni, arias, etc., by B. Luzzi, F. Sor, G. B. Peracchini, F. Tibaldi, G. Melia Romano, Manzoletto, etc., and anonymous; *circ.* 1816, etc. Part of 48347–8 belonged to Elizabeth Campbell in Rome, 1816.

Presented by Cecil Hopkinson, Esq.

48369. GUSTAV HOLST: first sketch of the Choral Fantasia, op. 51; *circ.* 1930. Condensed score. *Autograph.*

Presented by Miss Nora Day.

48590. MISCELLANEOUS VOLUME:

A. Fragments of choral music from a bookbinding (acquired in Austria) including fragments of Psalm settings, 'Salve Regina,' 'Die heiligen 5 Wunden'; early–late 17th cent.

Presented by Oliver Wray Neighbour, Esq.

E. Henry Russell: song, 'A cripple's ditty'; 19th cent. *Autograph.*

Presented by Sheridan Russell, Esq.

G. Beethoven: three-part canon, 'Ewig dein'; copied by C. F. Goffrie, *circ.* 1847.

Presented by Mrs. Florence Julia Street.

I. Thomas Lupo: letter to Mr. Cunningham requesting payment of his quarter's wages to George Hutcher; 2 Sept. 1618.

Sotheby's sale 12 Oct. 1954, lot 276.

K. Christoph Willibald von Gluck: letter to Franz Kruthoffer; 2 March 1778.

Sotheby's sale 12 Oct. 1954, lot 186.

1955

48595–7. SIR CHARLES SANTLEY: musical collections; 19th cent. As follows:

48595. Motets, songs, etc., by Santley. Mostly *autograph* and unpublished.

48596–7. Copies and arrangements by Santley of vocal works by Handel, Marcello, Niedermeyer, H. Purcell, Rossini, etc., and copies of music by H. Bedford, Benedict, P. Mazzoni, Sullivan, Verdi, Mendelssohn, Mercadante, Neukomm, Spohr, etc., owned by Santley.

Presented by the Royal Philharmonic Society (transferred from the Department of Printed Books).

1956

49196. DAME ETHEL SMYTH: notebook giving a list of her compositions, information relating to publications, etc.; *circ.* 1937.

Presented by Commander Lindsay R. Venn, R.N. (executor of Dame Ethel Smyth).

49286. LUIGI CHERUBINI: vocal compositions including 'Credo' à 8; 'Lungi da caro bene' (from 'Dorine', 1790); two arias from 'Alessandro nel Indie'; motet, 'Nemo gaudeat'; madrigal, 'Ninfa crudel', etc.; early 19th cent.

49287 B, C. FREDERICK EDWARD WEATHERLEY, two notebooks containing the words of songs, and libretti, including 'Olaf the Wild Huntsman'; 19th–20th cent. *Autograph.*

49288. FANNY KRUMPHOLZ, daughter of Johann Baptist Krumpholz, after-wards Mrs. Pittar: compositions and arrangements for the harp; early 19th cent. *Autograph*.

Transferred from the Department of Printed Books (Music Room).

49318. MISCELLANEOUS MUSIC, mostly *copies*, from the Gilbert Papers (Add. 49289–353) containing vocal parts of two numbers from 'Utopia Limited' (by Sullivan); part of the music to 'His Excellency' (by Frank Osmond Carr); instrumental parts for 'Rosencrantz and Guildenstern'; music manuscript book relating to 'Robert the Devil' (by Wilhelm Meyer Lutz); *autograph* song by Alfred J. Caldicott; late 19th cent.

49333. SIR ARTHUR SULLIVAN: draft song for 'The Gondoliers' (f. 63) and correspondence with Sir W. S. Gilbert (ff. 63–182); 1889–95.

49354. [ANTON?] STAMITZ: six string quartets (nos. 34–9 from a larger set); late 18th–early 19th cent. Parts, slightly imperfect.

Presented by Cecil Hopkinson, Esq.

49375–6. ITALIAN VOCAL MUSIC; 18th–19th cent. As follows:

  49375. Luigi Vecchiotti: 'Messa Breve a Quattro Voci' and a motet for tenor and orchestra, 'Qui venti subito insurgunt'; 19th cent. Scores.

  49376. Giovanni Paisiello, scena from 'Demetrio' and Guiseppe Giordani (Giordaniello), 'Le Tre Ore di Agonia di N.S.G.C.' for three voices and strings beg. 'Già trafitto in duro legno'; late 18th cent. Scores.

Presented by Mrs. Emily Cullum.

1957

49519. G. B. PERGOLESI: 'Salve Regina' and 'Stabat Mater' for voices with instrumental accompaniment: 18th cent.

Transferred from the Department of Printed Books (Music Room).

49527. WILLIAM BARCLAY SQUIRE, M.V.O.: papers as Honorary Curator of the King's Music Library, relating to his work on the *Catalogue of the King's Music Library*, Part I (The Handel Manuscripts), 1927, chiefly consisting of letters about Handel from Percy Robinson to Squire; 1922–6.

Transferred from the Department of Printed Books (Music Room).

49595. JOHN HENRY MAUNDER: 'Thor's War Song', chorus, with instrumental accompaniment; for alto, two tenor and bass voices; 19th cent. *Autograph.*

Presented by Messrs. Goodwin & Tabb, Ltd.

49597. MISCELLANEOUS VOLUME:

B (1). Max Reger: letter to ——; 23 Jan. 1914.

(2). Gustav Mahler: postcard to Gustav Lewy, theatre agent; 4 Apr. 1882.

Presented by Donald Mitchell, Esq.

O. Fragments of a polyphonic setting of the Mass taken from the binding of a copy of the *Legendae ad usum Sarum*, printed by Caxton, from St. Mary's Warwick; 15th cent.

Transferred from the Department of Printed Books.

1958

49599. SONATAS for various combinations of trumpets, oboes and strings, or strings alone, by D. Purcell, Eccles, Barrett, Bononcini, Finger, Paisible, Dieupart; early 18th cent. Parts.

Sotheby's sale 11 Dec. 1957, lot 510.

49600–3. PAPERS OF THE MUSICAL LEAGUE, founded in April 1908 'to foster the cause of music in England', etc.; 1908–13.

49600. Minute-book; 1908–13.

49601. List of members; 1908–13.

49602. Correspondence and papers including a few letters of Bax, Delius, Elgar, Grainger, Vaughan Williams, etc.; 1907–13.

49603. Programmes, articles and press cuttings on the Liverpool Festival of Sept. 1909; 1908–9.

49624–32. SIR WILLIAM HERSCHEL, the astronomer (1738–1822): symphonies; mid 18th cent. Partly *autograph.* As follows:

49624–7. Full scores of symphonies 1–18, 20–24.

49628–32. Parts of nos. 2–24.

Sotheby's sale 17 June 1958, lot 431.

49633–7. J. LESLIE STEPHEN: collections relating to the pianoforte. As follows:

49633. Records of journeys to secure data relating to the pianoforte export market; 1920–1.

49634–6. Notes and drawings relating to the construction of pianos; 1903–18.

49637. Historical notes on keyboard instruments, etc.; 20th cent.

Transferred from the Department of Printed Books.

49973–4. SIR EDWARD ELGAR: sketches of compositions, supplementing Add. MSS. 47900–8; 19th–20th cent. As follows:

49973A. Early works, arranged chronologically; 1872–*circ.* 1887. Viz: 'The Language of Flowers'; 'Chantant'; 'Stabat Mater' in F (tenor and bass parts only); hymn, 'By the Blood that flow'd from Thee'; 'Tantum Ergo' in D; 'While Shepherds watched', etc.; 'Salve Regina' in D; Credo in E minor, lacking much of the accompaniment; 'Wand of Youth', Suite no. 1, op. 1a; two polonaises in F and D minor for violin and piano, both imperfect; copies by Elgar of the Minstrels' entry from Wagner's 'Tannhäuser' and the Scherzo, op. 52, by Schumann; Powicke Quadrilles; fugue for oboe and violin, and fugue for organ; 'Sevillana', op. 7 (fragments); Offertorium in G, 'In Memoriam—W. A.'; 'O Salutaris Hostia' (two settings); 'Gloria' based on the second movement of Mozart's violin sonata, K. 547, etc.

49973B. Miscellaneous sketches, mostly only fragments, arranged chronologically; 1890–1908. Viz: 'My Love dwelt'; Étude Caractéristique, op. 24; 'Stars of the Summer Night', op. 23; Serenade for Strings, op. 20; 'The Black Knight', op. 25; 'O Happy Eyes', op. 18, no. 1; 'King Olaf', op. 30; 'Caractacus', op. 35; Enigma Variations, op. 36; 'Sea Pictures', op. 37; 'Dream of Gerontius', op. 38; 'Grania and Diarmid', op. 42; 'Weary Wind of the West'; sketches made at Rome, 1907, including 'Deep in my Soul', op. 53, no. 2, and 'O Wild West Wind', op. 53, no. 3; Christmas Greeting, op. 52 (with letters to Dr. G. R. Sinclair of Hereford relating to it), etc.

49974A. Sketches of the violin concerto, op. 61; before 1910.

49974B. Miscellaneous sketches; 1916–33. Viz: piano trio (unpublished); piano quintet in A minor, op. 84; 'cello concerto, op. 85; incidental music for 'Beau Brummel' (except the minuet); Severn Suite for brass band, op. 87; March in B flat; sonatina for piano, no. 2; printed edition of E. Pauer, *Hebrew Melodies* (Augener edition), the source of certain themes for 'The Apostles' and 'The Kingdom'. With a few photographs of Elgar, his birthplace and his father's shop in Worcester.

49974C. Notebook containing brief sketches; 1879–1933. Viz: violin concerto, op. 61; two items from the projected opera, 'Arden'; incidental music to Laurence Binyon's 'King Arthur'; 'The Apostles', Part

III'; 'Callicles', soprano scena; incidental music for 'Beau Brummel'; piano quintet in A minor, op. 84; 'Ozymandias', bass scena, 1917; 'Wand of Youth', Suite no. 2, op. 1b; 'The Spanish Lady', op. 89 (1).

49974D. Leather bound notebook, containing fragments of works never completed. Many leaves are torn out, the remaining contents are as follows: plan for an organ suite in F; sketch for the slow movement of a concerto in F; suite for strings in G; plan of a suite for strings in G, including a praelude, moresque and intermezzo, and ideas for 'Suite 2'; sonata, etc., for violin and piano; list of the original contents of the notebook.

Presented by Mrs. Carice Elgar Blake, daughter of the composer.

49977. MISCELLANEOUS VOLUME:

A. Thomas Ford: *signed* receipt to **Adam** Newton for his quarter's pension; 10 Apr. 1619.

Sotheby's sale 11 Dec. 1957, lot 570.

F. Dame Nellie Melba: facsimile of a farewell speech; 4 Sept. 1924.

Presented by L. C. Thomson, Esq.

N. Sir Arthur Sullivan: 'Allegro risoluto' in B flat minor for piano; 8 May 1866. *Autograph.*

Presented by Mrs. Carice Elgar Blake.

R. Covent Garden Theatre: single leaf from an account-book of expenses and receipts; 1817–18.

1959

49995. BERNARD VAN DIEREN: interlude from the 'Choral Symphony, based on poems from the Chinese', op. 11; copied by Peter Warlock, 20th cent. Score.

50071. MARY FRANCES BUMPUS: register of her songs, with notes of publications, terms, etc.; 1885–96.

Presented by J. G. Wilson, Esq., through the Guildhall Library.

50115. WILHELM FRIEDEMANN BACH: aria, 'Der Trost gehöret', for soprano with organ accompaniment; late 18th cent. Soprano and obligato organ parts. *Autograph.*

Sotheby's sale 12 May 1959, lot 369.

50122–9. DR. KARL ERICH ROEDIGER: collections for a catalogue of musical and liturgical manuscripts; 20th cent. As follows:

50122. Manuscripts at Erlangen.

50123–5. Thematic index of the above.

50126. Bamberg MSS.

50127. Nuremberg Museum.

50128. The State Library, Nuremberg.

50129. Index.

Presented by Mme K. E. Roediger and Dr. Alexander Roediger.

50138–9. KEYBOARD MUSIC; 18th cent. As follows:

50138. Sonatas by G. Masi, B. Lustrini, D. Paradies, Abbate L. de Rossi.
50139. Sonatas by N. Hadrava, Variations by Mozart, Partita by F. Urban.

Presented by Dr. Cecil Bernard Oldman, C.B.; C.V.O.

50140. RALPH VAUGHAN WILLIAMS: Symphony no. 4 in F minor; *circ.* 1935. Full score. *Autograph.*

Purchased with the assistance of the Ralph Vaughan Williams Trust.

50143. MISCELLANEOUS VOLUME:

F. Fragments of manuscript music found in the bindings of Add. MSS. 33694, 33705, 33709–11 (Skinner Journals) including the introduction in full score, to an Italian aria 'Se co . . . ', 18th cent.; fragment of a 'cello part in D?, 18th cent.; and *printed* fragments of Mozart and Meyerbeer.

1960

50144. MISCELLANEOUS INSTRUMENTAL MUSIC:

(1). Antoine Dauvergne: first violin part of the *Concerts de Simphonies*, opp. 3 and 4; 18th cent. ff. 1–17.

(2). Ferdinand Fränzl; two string quartets in C and A, op. 1, nos. 1 and 3; late 18th–early 19th cent. Parts. ff. 18–36b.

(3). Ladislav Dussek: Rondo for piano, 'Ma Barque Légère', arranged from an air by Grétry; early 19th cent. ff. 37b–41.

Transferred from the Department of Printed Books (Music Room). Presented by Cecil Hopkinson, Esq.

50151–72. HAROLD FRASER-SIMSON: musical compositions. As follows:

50151–4. 'Bonita'; *circ.* 1911. Full scores. *Autograph* and *copies.*

50155. 'The Maid of the Mountains'; *circ.* 1917. Full score. *Copy.*

50156. 'Southern Maid'; *circ.* 1917. Full score. *Copy.*

50157–8. 'Our Peg'; *circ.* 1919. Full score and vocal score. *Copies.*

50159. 'Street Singer'; *circ.* 1924. Full score. *Copy.*

50160. Fourteen songs from 'When we were very young'; before 1924. Piano score. *Autograph.*

50161. 'Betty in Mayfair'; *circ.* 1925. Full score. *Copy.*

50162–4. 'Venetian Wedding'; *circ.* 1926. Full score and piano score. Partly *autograph.*

50165–6. 'The Nightingale and the Rose'; *circ.* 1927. Full score and piano score. *Copies.*

50167. 'Toad of Toad Hall'; *circ.* 1930. Full score. *Copy.*

50168. 'Southern Maid'; 1920. *Printed* vocal score.

50169. 'Street Singer'; 1924. *Printed* vocal score.

50170. 'Maid of the Mountains'. Libretto. *Typewritten.*

50171. 'Southern Maid'. Libretto. *Typewritten.*

50172. 'Street Singer'. Libretto. *Typewritten.*

50151–67 *bequeathed by Mrs. Cicely Fraser-Simson;* 50168–72 *presented by Mrs. Ingram.*

50173–81. SIR ARNOLD BAX: musical compositions. *Autograph.* As follows:

50173–4. Festival Overture; 1909, 1911. Piano score and full score.

50175. Four Orchestral Pieces; 1912–3. Full score.

50176–7. 'The Happy Forest'; 13 May 1914, n.d. Piano score and full score.

50178. A Romance, for piano; before 1919.

50179. 'To the Name above Every Name'; 16 March 1923. Piano score.

50180. Sonata for 'cello and piano; 7 Nov. 1923.

50181. Song, 'Carry Clavel'; 6 Aug. 1925.

Presented by Miss Harriet Cohen, C.B.E.

50183. SIR GEORGE HENSCHEL: Sechs Clavierstücke, op. 30; 13–19 Dec. 1877. *Autograph.*

50185. VOCAL MUSIC, ARIAS, DUETS, ETC.: by Mozart, V. Rauzzini, L. da Bologna, T. Traetta, A. Boroni, G. Cocchi, *printed* duets by G. G. Ferrari, Rossini, etc.; early 19th cent. (watermark, 1798).

Presented by Dr. Cecil Bernard Oldman, C.B.; C.V.O.

50186. PETER WARLOCK (Philip Heseltine): six letters (including three *copies*) to Paul Ladmirault, 1925–30, *copy* of a letter from Bernard van Dieren to Ladmirault relating to Warlock's death, 1931, *copies* of letters from Ladmirault to his wife relating to the composition of 'La Prêtresse de Korydwen'; 1917–18.

Presented by Mme Ladmirault.

50187. LUIZ COSTA (b. 1879): piano quintet, op. 12, sonatina for violin and piano, op. 18, sonatina for violeta and piano, op. 19, sonatina for flute and piano, op. 23; 20th cent.

Transferred from the Department of Printed Books (Music Room).

50188. SIR EDWARD ELGAR: lectures as Richard Peyton Professor of Music at Birmingham University; 1905–8. *Typewritten.*

Presented by Mrs. Carice Elgar Blake.

50201. NATHANIEL GILES: service and anthems, together with an anthem by John Lugg; early 18th cent.

50202. JOHN SKELTON BUMPUS: letters to S. Royle Shore, and catalogue of his library; 1913, n.d.

50203. JOHN MUNDY: 'Psalms and Songs in 3, 4 and 5 parts'; 18th cent. *copy*, in score, from the printed part-books, *Songs and psalmes,* 1594, of this work.

50211–38. WILLIAM BAINES (1899–1922): *autograph* manuscripts of his musical compositions and other papers; 1911–22. The main contents are as follows:
    50211. Juvenile works: chants, hymn tunes; a waltz and march for orchestra; Humoresque for violin and piano; early piano pieces, including a march and fugue in C, a symphony in piano score, five waltzes, 'Reflections', 'Mountain Scenes'; 1911–14.
    50212. Juvenile works: chants; evening hymn; three songs to words by Nellie Nurton; piano trio in D minor, no. 1; Intermezzo for violin and piano, op. 2; Intermezzo for 'cello and piano, op. 3; Twelve Sketches for piano, op. 1; sonata in D minor; Four Nocturnes, op. 4; 'Melodie' in C for organ; 1913–15.

50213. Juvenile works: Two Characteristic Sketches for orchestra, op. 2a; Eight Pieces for piano, op. 2b; 1915–16.

50214. Juvenile works: anthem, 'Man's Dwelling-Place'; song, 'An Eastern Night'; three part-songs; piano trio in D minor (op. 1, no. 1, also called op. 7, no. 1) ; piano sonata in D minor, op. 3; Six Sketches for piano, op. 4; Prelude in C sharp major for piano; 'The Mulligan of Ballymulligan' for piano; 1916–17?

50215. Aubade for string quartet, op. 8b; violin sonata in G (original version); piano trio in D minor (op. 5, no. 2); piano pieces: Three Slumber Songs, op. 6, Five Pieces, op. 8a, Impression from 'Cherry Ripe', Four Miniature Tone Pictures, Three Impressions, op. 9; 1917.

50216–7. Symphony in C minor, op. 10, and related material; 1917.

50218. Two Songs, op. 12b; string quartet in E, op. 2; piano pieces: Two Elegies, op. 11, Three Playtime Sketches, op. 12a, sonata no. 2 in A minor, op. 13, Six Pieces, op. 14, 'A Mood', 'Passion of Destiny', 'Roccoco'; 1917–18.

50219. Hymn tune; piano trio in D minor (one movement condensed from the trio in 50215); Two Pieces and Romance in F for 'cello and piano; piano pieces: Six Dream Impressions, op. 16, Four Sketches, sonata in F sharp minor, op. 4; 1918.

50220. Song, 'Nights of Music'; orchestral Andante in A minor; 'The Island of the Fay' for orchestra; violin sonata in G (revised); 'Rain Splash' for 'cello and piano; piano pieces: 'Paradise Gardens', Poem in B, op. 6, no. 2, Introduction and Valse, op. 3, no. 1, 'A Moon Wander', Concert Study in A minor, op. 6, no. 3, Seven Preludes, 'Dead Heart Flower', 'The Little Wavelets', 'O Cuckoo', 'The Island of the Fay', Four Poems, February Pastoral; 1918–19.

50221. Five songs; string quartet piece in C; 'Marionettes' for violin and piano; piano pieces: sonata in F sharp minor, 'Vale of Memories'; 1919.

50222. 'Little Imps' for orchestra; Rhapsody in F sharp minor for string quartet; string orchestra piece, Prelude to a Doll's Ballet; 'Dream Temple' for violin and piano; piano pieces: 'Coloured Leaves', Three Concert Studies, 'Milestones', Prelude in D flat, Cyril Scott Fragment, 'Silverpoints', 'Tides', Prelude and Seven Diversions for two pianos; 1918–21.

50223. 'Thought Drift' for orchestra; two pieces and Andante for string quartet; piano pieces: Twilight Pieces, 'Poème de concert', and version for piano and orchestra, Prelude-Filigree, 'Idyll', 'Pictures of Light', 'A Last Sheaf', Eight Preludes; 1921.

50224. Musical sketches.

50225. Literary works.

50226–30. Diaries, 1918–22.

50231. Biographical notes.

50232–3. Correspondence.

50234. Press cuttings.

50235. Programmes.

50236. Posters.

50237. Miscellaneous printed matter.

50238. Photographs.

Partly bequeathed by Mrs. Mary Baines, mother of the composer, and partly presented by Robert Keys, Esq., and Mervyn Roberts, Esq.

50253. FRANZ SCHUBERT: wind parts of the 'Salve Regina' in F, originally written for soprano, orchestra and organ; copied by Ferdinand Schubert, brother of the composer, 29 Jan. 1823.

50262–74. GIULIO COTTRAU: musical works; 19th–20th cent. Partly *autograph*. As follows:

50262–4. 'Griselda'. Orchestral parts, Prelude in full score, 'Festa da Ballo' from Act I, *printed* vocal score, 1878, with *autograph* corrections.

50265. 'La Lega Lombarda'; before 1891. Full score.

50266–7. 'Cordelia'; before 1913. Orchestral parts and *printed* vocal score with *autograph* corrections.

50268. 'Pericle'; before 1916. Full scores, etc.

50269. 'Giovanna d' Arco'; 20th cent. Full scores, etc.

50270. Songs, in an album.

50271. Miscellaneous music.

50272. Libretti and scenarios.

50273. Press cuttings relating to 'Griselda' and 'Cordelia' in an album.

50274. Letters relating to copyright, mainly from Mme Cottrau; 20th cent.

Presented by F. W. Hall, Esq.

50359. JOHANN CHRISTOPH PEPUSCH: 'A Short Treatise on Harmony'; after 1730. Copied from an edition by John Walsh.

Presented by the Rev. H. F. Shepherd.

50360. MAURICE RAVEL: letters to Ralph Vaughan Williams; 1908–19. *French.*
Presented by Mrs. Ursula Vaughan Williams.

50361–482. RALPH VAUGHAN WILLIAMS COLLECTION. *Autograph* music manuscripts; 1896–1958. As follows:

SYMPHONIES

50361–6. A Sea Symphony; 1903–9. Sketches, *printed* proofs of vocal score, full score, *printed* full score with *autograph* corrections.

50367–8. A London Symphony; 1913. Sketches and piano scores.

50369. Pastoral Symphony; 1916–21. Full score.

50370. Symphony no. 4 in F minor; 1931–4. Two-piano scores.

50371–2. Symphony no. 5 in D major; 1938–43. Early sketches, two-piano scores, and full score.

50373–4. Symphony no. 6 in E minor; 1944–7. Sketches and two-piano scores.

50375. Sinfonia Antartica; 1949–52. Sketches, etc.

50376–7. Symphony no. 8 in D minor; 1953–5. Sketches and rough full score.

50378–84. Symphony no. 9 in E minor; 1956–7. Sketches, piano score, early full score and final full score.

CONCERTOS, etc.

50385. Piano concerto; 1926–31. Full score.

50386. Suite for viola; 1934. Full score.

50387–8. Oboe concerto; 1944. Early sketches and full score.

50389. Romance for harmonica; 1952. Full score.

50390–2. Tuba concerto; 1954. Sketches and full scores.

SMALLER INSTRUMENTAL WORKS

50393. Prelude and Fugue in C minor; 1921–30. Full score.

50394–5. 'The Running Set'; 1936. Two-piano scores, full score and parts.

50396. A Folk Dance Medley and March Suite 'founded on English Folktunes'; n.d. Short score.

50397. Two Hymn Tune Preludes; 1936. Full score.

50398–9. Household Music; 1941. Full score and parts.

50400. Suite for two pipes with 'Canzona' for three pipes; n.d. Scores, etc.

50401. Prelude on an Old Carol Tune; 1953. Full score.

50402. Prelude on Three Welsh Hymn Tunes; 1955. Full score and *printed copy*.

50403. Two Organ Preludes; 1956. Score.

50404–5. Variations for Brass Band; 1957. Scores and sketches.

OPERAS, BALLETS AND MASQUES

50406. 'Hugh the Drover'; 1910–14. Fragments and discards, with a *printed copy*.

50407–8. 'On Christmas Night'; 1921. Full scores.

50409–10. 'Sir John in Love'; 1924–30. Full scores and libretto.

50411. 'Job'; 1930. Opening of a score for two pianos.

50412–15. 'The Poisoned Kiss'; 1927–9, etc. Sketches and full scores.

50416–17. 'Riders to the Sea'; 1925–32. Rough score and full score.

50418–20. 'Pilgrim's Progress'; 1909–52. Two early versions and revised full score.

50421. 'The Bridal Day'; 1938–9, etc. Full score.

FILM MUSIC AND INCIDENTAL MUSIC.

50422–3. '49th Parallel'; 1940–1; Sketches, full scores of the film music and the suite.

50424–6. 'Coastal Command'; 1942. Sketches, full score of the suite.

50427–8. 'The People's Land'; 1941?–3. Sketches and full score.

50429–30. 'The Story of a Flemish Farm'; 1943. Sketches, full score and control score of the film music, full score of the suite.

50431. 'Scott of the Antarctic'; 1948. A few sketches.

50432. Incidental music to 'Richard II'; 1944.

50433. Incidental music to 'The Mayor of Casterbridge'; 1951.

OTHER VOCAL WORKS

50434–5. 'Willow wood'; 1903, 1908. Piano score and full score.

50436. 'Sound Sleep'; 1903, 1910. Full score.

50437. 'Silent Noon'; 1905. Full score and parts.

50438. 'Songs of Travel', Book I; 1905. Full scores of the orchestrated version.

50439. 'Toward the Unknown Region'; 1906. Full score.

50440. Five Mystical Songs; 1911. Vocal score, etc.

50441. Fantasia on Christmas Carols; 1912. Full score.

50442. 'O clap your Hands'; 1920. Full score.

50443–4. Mass in G minor; 1920–1. Organ part, full score.

50445–6. 'Sancta Civitas'; 1925. Full score and voice parts.

50447. 'Benedicite'; 1929. Full score.

50448. Two of Three Choral Hymns; 1929. Scores.

50449. The Hundredth Psalm; 1929. Full score.

50450. 'In Windsor Forest'; 1929. Full score.

50451–2. 'Magnificat'; 1932. Two full scores.

50453–4. 'Dona Nobis Pacem'; 1936. Vocal score and full score.

50455–7. 'Five Tudor Portraits'; 1935. Sketches, vocal score and full score.

50458. 'Nothing is here for Tears'; 1936. Full scores.

50459. 'Festival Te Deum'; 1937. Full score.

50460. 'Flourish for a Coronation'; 1937. Vocal score and full score.

50461. 'All hail the Power'; 1938. Full score.

50462–3. Six Choral Songs; 1940. Vocal score and full score.

50464. 'England, my England'; 1941. Three scores with accompaniment for piano, orchestra or military band.

50465. The Airmen's Hymn; 1942. Rough vocal and full score.

50466. A Song of Thanksgiving; 1944. Full score.

50467. 'The Voice out of the Whirlwind'; 1947. Full score.

50468. Folksongs of the Four Seasons; 1949. Full score.

50469. Fantasia on the Old 104th; 1949. Full score.

50470–2. 'The Sons of Light'; 1950. Sketches and full scores.

50473–4. An Oxford Elegy; 1949–52. Voice parts, vocal scores, full scores.

50475. The Old Hundredth; 1953. Vocal score and full score.

50476. 'Te Deum' and 'Benedictus', 1954. Vocal score.

50477. 'Hodie'; 1953–4. Full score.

50478. 'Sun, Moon, Stars, and Man'; 1954. Full score.

50479. 'Epithalamium'; 1957. Vocal and full scores.

50480. Miscellaneous small vocal works: 'How can the Tree'; 1896. Full score;–'Orpheus with his Lute'; 1901. Full score;–'Is it Nothing to you' ('O vos omnes'); 1922. Rough vocal score;–'Motion and Stillness'; 1922. Vocal score;–'The Jolly Carter'; 1925. Full score;–Six English Folksongs; 1935. Vocal score;–Three Old German Songs; 1937. Vocal score;–'The Willow Whistle'; *circ.* 1939;–The New Commonwealth'; 1943. Full score;–Hymn for St. Margaret; 1948. Two vocal scores;–

'The Vagabond'; 1952. Vocal score;-'In the Spring'; 1952. Vocal score;-'God bless the Master'; 1956. Vocal score;-'I have trod'. Vocal score;-Carols, mostly unaccompanied.

50481. Miscellaneous vocal works: Three Shakespeare Songs; 1951. Vocal score;-Seven songs from the 'Pilgrim's Progress'; 1952. Vocal score;-Eight Housman Songs; 1954;-Ten Blake Songs; 1957;-Three vocalises for soprano and clarinet; 1958.

50482. Two Sketchbooks including sketches for 'Riders to the Sea', Piano Concerto, 'Job', 'Belshazzar'; sketches for the Tuba Concerto, 'Pilgrim's Progress' and 'Hodie'.

Presented by Mrs. Ursula Vaughan Williams, widow of the composer.

50483. MISCELLANEOUS VOLUME:

D. Edward Moore Sheehan: sketches for his second set of waltzes; 19th–20th cent. *Autograph.*

Presented by Harold J. Sheehan, Esq.

E. Charles François Gounod: letter to Mrs. Helen Wesché; 25 Apr. 1878.

Presented by Edward Croft-Murray, Esq.

O. Jules Massenet: letter to Giulio Cottrau; 31 Jan. 1888. *French.*

Presented by F. W. Hall, Esq.

S. Two suites in tablature for mandora lute, formerly bound with a printed copy of Wolf Heckel, *Lautten Büch, von mancherley schönen vnd lieblichen stucken* . . . , Strasburg, 1562 (Hirsch III. 326); early 18th cent.

Transferred from the Department of Printed Books (Music Room).

V. Petr Ilich Tchaikovsky: letter to the pianist, Anna Yakovlevna Levenson; 15 Apr. 1881. *Russian* with *English* translation.

1961

50490–5. BENJAMIN DALE: musical compositions. *Autograph.* As follows:

50490. Piano sonata in D minor (first movement); [1902].

50491 A, B. Suite for viola and piano, consisting of Maestoso and Romance; 1906.

50492. Romance for viola and orchestra (cf. 50491 B); 1909. Full score.

50493. Miscellaneous: 'Night Fancies' for piano; 1907;-A Hymn of the Nativity, for voices and orchestra; n.d. Vocal score with piano accompaniment;-'A Dirge of Love', op. 8, no. 2, from 'Twelfth Night', for voice, viola and piano; 1911;-Song, 'Carpe Diem' beginning 'O Mistress mine'; 1918;-English Dance for violin and piano; 1919;-'A Holiday Tune' for violin and piano; 1920.

50494. Sonata for violin and piano, op. 11; 1921-2.

50495. A Song of Praise, for chorus and orchestra; 1923. Full score.

Presented by Mrs. Margit Dale, widow of the composer.

50496-505. CALVOCORESSI COLLECTION. Musical *autographs* formerly owned by Michel Dmitri Calvocoressi; 20th cent. As follows:

50496. Béla Bartók: Hungarian folksongs; early 20th cent. One leaf. *Autograph.*

50497. Frederick Delius: Dance for harpsichord, 1919, and part of the 'Hassan' music (two leaves), *circ.* 1920. *Autograph.* With a *copy* of the song, 'Weinrosen' (composed 1897), in the hand of Mrs. Delius.

50498. Bernard Van Dieren: string quartet; [1928]. *Autograph.*

50499. Paul Ladmirault: 'Printemps' and 'Deux Mélodies'; 1902, 1908. *Autograph.*

50500. Sergei Liapunov: Tarentelle for piano, op. 25; 1906. *Autograph.*

50501. Willem Pijper: sonata for flute and piano; 1924-5. *Autograph.*

50502. George Poniridy: Deux Mélodies Arméniennes; n.d. *Autograph.*

50503. Joseph Marie Déodat de Séverac: 'À Cheval dans la Prairie' for piano; 1904. *Autograph.*

50504. Alexandre Tansman: 'cello sonata; n.d. [1930]. *Autograph.*

50505. Miscellaneous *autographs*: Louis Aubert: song, 'Crépuscules d'Automne'; 1908;-Bernard Van Dieren: song, 'Weeping and Kissing' beg. 'A kiss I begged'; *copy*, dated 22 May 1930;-Gabriel Dupont: piano music; n.d. [before 1906];-Aleksandr Glazunov: arrangement of Russian folksong; n.d.;-Petro Petridis: Suite Grecque (first page only of the second movement, Pastorale); [*circ.* 1929];-Erik Satie: 'Prélude de la Porte Héroïque du Ciel'; n.d. Orchestrated by Roland Manuel. Full score, in the hand of Roland Manuel;-Peter Warlock: song, 'Rutterkin'; 1922;-Egon Wellesz: Persisches Ballett, op. 30; n.d. [produced 1924]. Full score (*imperfect*).

Presented by Miss Ethel Glave in accordance with the wishes of her late aunt, Mrs. Calvocoressi.

50529. RUTLAND BOUGHTON: letters to George Bernard Shaw; 1912-45.

Bequeathed by George Bernard Shaw, Esq.

50662. GEORGE BERNARD SHAW: musical articles; 1885–1925. Partly *autograph*.

50752. JOHN CURWEN (1816–80), founder of the Tonic Sol-fa method and of J. Curwen & Sons: notebook containing notes and essays on philosophy; before 1836.

Presented by Messrs. John Curwen & Sons, Ltd.

50753. FRIEDRICH HARTMANN GRAF (1727–95), flautist and Director of Music at Augsburg: four letters and other documents, including a letter of Johann Conrad von Fingerlin, relating to music at Augsburg; 1781–3.

50756–87. MUSIC MANUSCRIPTS OF ENGLISH COMPOSERS; late 19th–20th cent. *Autograph* unless otherwise stated. As follows:

50756. W. G. Alcock: 'When the Lord turned', anthem; March 1912. Full score.

50757. Sir I. Atkins: Hymn of Faith; [1905]. Full score.

50758. Sir Granville Bantock: 'The Great God Pan'; 1915. Full score.

50759A, B. Sir J. Barnby: 'Magnificat' (*autograph*) and 'Nunc Dimittis' (*copy*); n.d. Full score.

50760. Sir A. H. Brewer: 'The Holy Innocents'; 1904 revised 1922. Full score. Partly *autograph*.

50761. Sir A. H. Brewer: Three Elizabethan Pastorals; 1906. Full score.

50762. Sir J. F. Bridge: 'Blessed be the Lord'; 1897. Full score. Partly *autograph*.

50763. S. Coleridge-Taylor: 'The Soul's Expression', op. 42; [*circ.* 1900]. Full score.

50764. S. Coleridge-Taylor: 'The Blind Girl of Castel Cuillé', op. 43; [1901]. Full score.

50765. S. Coleridge-Taylor: 'Sons of the Sea'; n.d. Full score.

50766. Sir Henry Coward: 'Bethany', cantata; 24 Feb. 1891. Full score.

50767. Sir Frederic H. Cowen: 'The Water Lily'; 1892. Full score.

50768. Alan Gray: 'The Legend of the Rock Buoy Bell', ballad for chorus and orchestra; 16 Nov. 1892. Full score.

50769. Basil Harwood: Concerto for Organ; June 1910. Full score.

50770. Sir George Henschel: Der CXXX Psalm; 20 May 1874. Full score.

50771. Henry Festing Jones: 'King Bulbous'; *circ.* 1896. Full score.

50772. Charles Harford Lloyd: 'Andromeda'; 7 Sept. 1886. Full score.

50773A, B. Sir George Macfarren: 'The Lady of the Lake'; 31 Jan. 1876. Full score. *Copy*.

50774. Sir Alexander Mackenzie: 'Lochinvar', op. 2; n.d. Full score.

50775. Sir Alexander Mackenzie: 'Highland Ballad', op. 47, no. 1; 1891. Full score.

50776. Charles Macpherson: Solemn Thanksgiving and 'Te Deum'; 1919. Full score.

50777. Sir Stanley Marchant: 'Te Deum'; 1937. Full score. *Copy* with *autograph?* notes.

50778. Sir George Clement Martin: 'Out of the Deep'; 1901. Full score.

50779. Ebenezer Prout: 'Damon and Phintias'; *circ.* 1889. Full score.

50780. Sir Arthur Somervell: 'The Forsaken Merman'; 7 Sept. 1893. Full score.

50781. Dr. T. L. Southgate: collections relating to the lyra viol manuscript in the Henry Watson Music Library, Manchester; early 20th cent.

50782. Sir John Stainer: 'Lord, thou art God'; n.d. Full score.

50783A, B. Charles Steggall: 'Cantate' and 'Deus Misereatur', 'Magnificat' and 'Nunc Dimittis'; 1878, 1881. Full scores.

50784. Ernest Walker: Hymn to Dionysius; Jan. 1906. Full score.

50785. John E. West: 'Light's glittering Morn'; n.d. Full score. Partly *autograph?*

50786. Charles Wood: 'Ode to the West Wind'; [1890]. Full score.

50787. Baldassare Galuppi; 'Gloria' à 4; 18th cent. Full score. *Copy.*

Presented by Novello & Co., Ltd.

50790–820. ERNST VON DOHNÁNYI: *autograph* musical compositions, etc.; *circ.* 1888–1960. As follows:

JUVENILE WORKS

50790. Piano works: Two Études in D and C;-Three Bagatelles in C sharp minor, D and A minor;-Tarantella in E minor;-Mazurka in C;-Impromptu in A;-Scherzo in A;-Walzer in C sharp minor;-Pastorale in A minor; 1888;-Tarantella in E minor; 1888;-Scherzino in A minor; 1888;-Zwei kleine Scherzandos in E minor and G; 1888;-Two Mazurkas in B flat minor and B flat; 1889;-Sechs Fantasiestücke; 1890;-Impromptu in E; 1890;-Sonata in A; 1890;-Sonata in G minor; 1890;-Tarantella in C minor; 1890;-Sonata movement in B flat;-Canon in C;-Bagatelle in D; 1890;-Romance in A minor; 1891;-Fantasiestück in A; 1891;-Pièces sur le nom 'Heda'; 1891;-Novelette in E; 1891;-Fantasie for organ in C minor; 1892;-Impromptu in F minor; 1892;-Romance in F sharp; 1894.

50791. Early violin pieces: Six short pieces with piano, Adagio in A, etc., with piano, Piece in G for two violins; 1895;-Early 'cello pieces: Allegro vivace in D minor, with piano, Andante and Allegro in D, with piano;-Early piano quintet in B flat;-Early string quintet in G.

50792. Sonatas in G and C for 'cello and piano; 1888, 1889;-Two string quartets in D and G minor; 1889, 1890.

50793. Piano quartet in F sharp minor; 1891-3.

50794. Overture in B flat for orchestra; 1892;-Third string quartet in A minor; 1893;-String quartet in D minor; 1893;-String sextet; 1893.

50795. Songs: Fragment of an opera, 'Die Bergknappen'; 1891;-'Zu deinen Füssen'; 1891;-'Die verlassene Fischersbraut'; 1892;-Zwei Liedchen; 1892;-'Das verlassene Mägdlein'; 1892;-'Du schönes Fischermädchen'; 1892;-'Das Blumenmädchen'; 1892;-'Wie dunkel und still'; 1892;-'Wilder Ritt'; 1892;-'Reue'; 1893;-'Ich sehe wie in einem Spiegel'; 1893;-'Auf Wiedersehen'; 1894;-Duet, 'Ein Blick in deine Augen'; 1894.

50796. Sacred music: 'Ave Maria'; 1891;-Mass in C; 1892;-'Pater Noster'; 1892;-'O Salutaris Hostia' and 'Ave Verum'; 1893;-'Veni Sancte Spiritus'; 1893;-'Kyrie';-Király hymnus;-Sixth Psalm.

LATE WORKS

50797. 'Cantus vitae', op. 38; 1940.

50798A–C. Suite en Valse, op. 39; 1942-7.

50799A, B. Second piano concerto, op. 42; 1947.

50800. Second violin concerto, op. 43; 1949-50.

50801. Three Singular Pieces for piano, op. 44; 1951.

50802. Concertino for harp and orchestra, op. 45; 1952.

50803. 'Stabat Mater', op. 46; 1953.

50804. American Rhapsody, op. 47; 1953.

50805A, B. Daily Finger Exercises; 1960?

50806A, B. Sketches and smaller works including the Aria, op. 48, no. 1.

BIOGRAPHICAL MATERIAL

50807A, B. Miscellaneous papers in *Hungarian* and *German,* including four letters to his father, 1896-1901, radio scripts, photostats of political documents.

50808. Notebook recording dates of composition and performances of early works; 1888-96. *German.*

50809-10. Original draft in *Hungarian* and *printed* copy (translated by Ilona von Dohnányi) of *Message to Posterity from Ernst von Dohnányi,* 1960.

50811–12. Biography of Dohnányi by Ilona von Dohnányi. *Typewritten.*

50813–15. Photographs.

50816–18. Press cuttings.

50819. Beethoven, *Sonaten für Pianoforte* (Peter's edition): Dohnányi's copy with his fingerings.

50820. Doctor of Music Diploma of Florida State University awarded to Dohnányi on 1 June 1957.

Presented by Mrs. Ilona von Dohnányi, widow of the composer.

50822. HOWARD ELLIS CARR (1880–1960): two symphonies; *circ.* 1903–5. Full scores. *Autograph.*

Presented by Lloyds Bank, Ltd., as executors of the composer.

50823. PERCY ALDRIDGE GRAINGER: piano arrangement of 'Country Gardens'; 1918. *Autograph.*

Presented by Mrs. Ella Grainger.

50828. VINCENZO BELLINI: aria, 'A tanto duol quest' anima' from the opera, 'Bianca e Fernando'; 19th cent. *Copy.*

Presented by Mrs. Violet Bridgewater.

50843. RALPH VAUGHAN WILLIAMS: 'Hugh the Drover'; 1911–14. Vocal score. *Autograph.*

Presented by Sir Steuart Wilson.

50845. ALBUM OF SONGS, with piano accompaniment, by Bishop, Pleyel, arrangements from Handel, Mozart, etc., traditional and national airs, and anonymous; probably copied by Eliza Lane and dated 30 Jan. 1819.

Transferred from the Department of Printed Books (Music Room).

50846. STEPHEN STORACE: duet, 'Sweet little Barbara', from 'The Iron Chest', with two anonymous duets; owned by Eliza Lane, 11 July 1816.

Transferred from the Department of Printed Books (Music Room).

50849. MISCELLANEOUS VOLUME:

A. François Danzi (1763–1826): 4ᵉ 'Duo pour Alto et Violoncelle'; early 19th cent. Two parts.

Transferred from the Department of Printed Books (Music Room).

C. Sir Henry Bishop: glee, 'Hark! Apollo strikes the Lyre'; *circ.* July 1842. *Copy* with *autograph* note.

Presented by Messrs. John Curwen & Sons, Ltd.

D. Vincent Novello: two letters to T. Severn; 14 Dec. 1841, 6 Sept. 1842.

Presented by Sir Stanley Unwin through the Friends of the National Libraries.

J. Sir Arthur Bliss: letter to A. Hyatt King; 20 May 1961.

Transferred from the Department of Printed Books (Music Room).

N. Miscellaneous music, including an *autograph* song by C. J. Bond, *circ.* 1874, *copies* of songs by G. Herbert Bond, M. Coco, F. Allitsen, polka by Johann Strauss, waltzes and Neapolitan songs by F. Rehfeld and G. Prisco; 19th cent.

Presented by Miss Nicola Speed.

1962

50850. MISCELLANEOUS VOLUME:

B. Notebook mainly relating to the folksong, 'Lubin'; 20th cent.

Presented by Noel Teulon-Porter, Esq.

L. Sir Edward Elgar: letter to Rutland Boughton; 1899.

50852. WILLIAM BARCLAY SQUIRE: letters to him from musical scholars including G. E. P. Arkwright, Sir G. Grove, F. Kidson, O. Sonneck; 19th–20th cent.

Transferred from the Department of Printed Books (Music Room).

50856. FRAGMENTS OF MUSIC formerly bound in a Ripon Cathedral book: 'A Ballet of ye deth of ye Cardynall' beginning 'I herde a voce rewfully complane'; 16th cent. Three voice parts in choir-book score. Two stanzas.

Transferred from the Department of Printed Books.

50859. BASS PART-BOOK OF SERVICES AND ANTHEMS by Blow, Humfrey, H. Purcell, Aldrich, Child, Byrd, Tallis; late 17th cent.

Sotheby's sale 9 April 1962, lot 105.

50860. BASS PART-BOOK OF ANTHEMS by Humfrey, Blow, Turner, H. Purcell, Locke, Tudway; late 17th cent.

Sotheby's sale 9 April 1962, lot 105.

50861. GRATTAN COOKE: Fantasia for oboe with piano accompaniment; 1828.
Autograph?

Sotheby's sale 9 April 1962, lot 105.

50862. RALPH VAUGHAN WILLIAMS: 'Household Music'; 1942. Full score
Autograph.

Presented by Mrs. Ursula Vaughan Williams, by courtesy of Harry Blech, Esq.

50863. RALPH VAUGHAN WILLIAMS: Romance for viola; n.d. *Copy* in the hand
of Vaughan Williams's first wife, Adeline.

Presented by Mrs. Ursula Vaughan Williams.

50867–87. PERCY ALDRIDGE GRAINGER: musical manuscripts, etc.; 1898–1957.
Autograph. As follows:

ORIGINAL WORKS

50867–9. 'Hill-Song I'; 1901, 1921–3. Full scores of the original and revised
versions, and orchestral parts of the revised version.

50870. 'Hill-Song II'; 1907. Full score.

50871–6. Kipling settings:

> 50871. The Ballad of the 'Bolivar'; 1901;-The Ballad of the 'Clam-
> pherdown'; 1899;-'Soldier, Soldier'; 1899, 1907–8.

> 50872–3. 'The Widow's Party'; 1906–39.

> 50874–5. Morning Song in the Jungle; 1905;-'Tiger-Tiger'; 1905;-
> 'The Inuit'; 1902;-'The Peora Hunt'; 1906;-'The Fall of the Stone';
> n.d.;-'The Only Son'; 1945–7;-Incomplete orchestral parts of 'The
> Peora Hunt', 'Mowgli's Song against People', and 'The Fall of the
> Stone'.

> 50876. 'The Running of Shindand'; 1901–4;-'Northern Ballad'; 1898,
> 1899;-'Ride with an idle Whip'; 1899;-'The Men of the Sea'; 1899;-
> Anchor Song; 1899, 1915;-'We have fed our Sea'; 1900–11;- 'The
> Sea-Wife'; 1947.

50877–8. 'Mock Morris'; 1910.

50879. Miscellaneous: sketches for a Dance added, at Delius's request,
to his 'Hassan' music; 1923;- English Dance for orchestra and organ
(alto saxophone part only); n.d;-English Waltz; 1899–1945;-'When the
World was young'; 1950.

ARRANGEMENTS

50880–3. British Folk Music Settings:

50880. 'The Sussex Mummers' Christmas Carol', setting no. 2; 1905–57;-'Brigg Fair' (sketch only), setting no. 7;-'I'm seventeen come Sunday', setting no. 8; 1905–12;-'Died for Love', setting no. 10; 1906–7;-'Six Dukes', setting no. 11; n.d.

50881–2. 'Shepherd's Hey', setting no. 20; 1908–13.

50883. 'Country Gardens', setting no. 22; 1919–53;-'The Sprig of Thyme', setting no. 24; 1920;-'Green bushes', setting no. 25; 1921.

50884. Other folk music settings: 'Bristol Town'; 1906–47;-'The Duke of Marlborough'; 1905–9;-'Lisbon'; 1943;-'Willow, Willow'; 1902–11;-Miscellaneous sketches.

50885–6. Arrangements for two pianos of English Dance by Balfour Gardiner and Dance Rhapsody, no. 1, by Delius; 1925, 1922.

LITERARY

50887. Draft article, 'Collecting with the Phonograph', published in the *Journal of the Folk-Song Society*, 1908, with *printed* proof.

Presented by Mrs. Ella Grainger, widow of the composer.

50888–900. CHURCH HOUSE MANUSCRIPTS: hymn books, etc., from Church House, Westminster; 18th–19th cent. As follows:

50888. Anonymous psalms, hymns, parts of services, etc.; early 18th cent. Possibly compiled by 'R.S.B^n: 18 July 1718'.

50889. Psalms, canons, hymns, etc., probably compiled by George Holtam; 1744, 1758, etc.

50890. 'A Collection of Psalm-Tunes selected from several eminent Authors. By John Greenwood.' Includes extracts from Dr. C. Gibbons, Boyce, H. Purcell, Croft; mid 18th cent.

50891. Two books of psalm tunes by J. Darwall, Vicar of Walsall; 1783. Mostly *autograph*.

50892. Psalm tunes by Dr. B. Cooke, Croft, Handel, etc.; late 18th cent.

50893. 'Norwich Tabernacle Book': hymn tunes; 1st half 19th cent.

50894. Hymn tunes by J. Battishill, J. Kemp, G. W. Chard, W. Jackson, W. Marsh; 1813, etc.

50895. Chants 'as sung at Lichfield Cathedral', by Rev. Thomas Helmore: 6 March 1841. *Autograph*.

50896. Transcriptions by Christina Rachel Bird of songs by C. E. Horn, Beethoven, Arne, Bishop, etc.; 1852–8, etc.

50897. Edwin George Monk: chants; 1857–60. *Autograph.*

50898. Chants by various composers mostly of the 18th cent.; after 1840.

50899. 'A Course of Anthems, Introits, Hymns at the Offertory, and after Evening Service, throughout the Year'; mid 19th cent.

50900. Collection of *autograph* hymn tunes by numerous English composers mostly of the late 19th cent.

Transferred from the Department of Printed Books (Music Room).

50960–51012. RUTLAND BOUGHTON: musical works; 1895–1952. *Autograph.* As follows:

MUSIC-DRAMAS

50960. 'Eolf'; 1903. Vocal score.

50961–2. 'The Birth of Arthur'; 1908–9. Vocal score and fragments of full score.

50963. 'The Immortal Hour'; 1912–14. Full score.

50964–5. 'The Round Table'; 1915–16. Vocal and full scores.

50966. 'Bethlehem'; 1915. Full score.

50967–8. 'Alkestis'; 1920–4. Vocal and full scores (original and revised versions).

50969–70. 'The Queen of Cornwall'; 1923–5. Vocal and full scores.

50971–2. 'The Ever Young'; 1928–9. Vocal and full scores.

50973–4. 'The Lily Maid'; 1933–4. Vocal and full scores.

50975–7. 'Galahad'; 1904–44. Full score of 'The Chapel in Lyonesse' (afterwards the second scene in 'Galahad') and libretto, vocal and full scores of 'Galahad'.

50978–9. 'Avalon'; 1944–5. Libretto, vocal and full scores.

BALLETS AND INCIDENTAL MUSIC

50980–1. 'Snow White'; 1912. Condensed and full scores.

50982. 'The Death of Columbine'; 1921. Full score.

50983. 'May Day'; 1926–7. Condensed and imperfect full scores.

50984. Music for 'The Little Plays of St Francis'; 1924–5.

ORCHESTRAL WORKS

50985. Cromwell Symphony; 1904. Full score.

50986. Deirdre (or Celtic) Symphony; 1927. Full score.

50987. Symphony no. 3 in B minor; 1937. Full score.

50988. 'A Summer Night'; 1899–1903. Full score.

50989. Purcell Variations; 1901. Full score.

50990. 'Troilus and Cressida'; 1902. Full score.

50991. 'Love and Spring'; 1906. Full score.

50992. 'Three Flights'; 1929. Full score.

50993. Four English Pieces; 1937. Full score.

50994. Reunion Variations; 1945. Full score.

50995. 'Three Aylesbury Games'; 1952. Full score.

50996. Small orchestral works: Grand March from 'The Bride of Messina'; *circ.* 1897, *presented by Michael Hurd, by courtesy of Mrs. E. Jenkins*;- 'Winter Sun'; 1933;-Chorale Suite arranged from Bach Choral Preludes; *circ.* 1941;-Rondo in Wartime; 1940–1;-Prelude on Christmas Hymn; 1941.

50997. Concerto no. 1 in C minor for oboe and strings; 1936. Full score.

50998. Concerto no. 2 in G minor for oboe and strings; 1936–7. Full score.

50999. Concerto for flute and strings; 1937. Imperfect condensed and full scores.

51000–1. Concerto for trumpet and orchestra; 1943. Condensed and full scores.

CHAMBER MUSIC

51002. String quartet no. 1 in A; 1923.

51003. String quartet no. 2 in F; 1923.

51004. Oboe quartet no. 2; 1945.

51005. Smaller chamber works: Dorian Study; 1920–3?;-'Winter Sun'; 1933;-'Somerset Pastoral' and the 'Passing of the Fairy'; 1937;-Trio for violin, 'cello and piano; 1948;-Three Songs without Words for oboe quartet; 1950.

VOCAL WORKS

51006. Works for voice and orchestra: 'Standing beyond Time'; 1907;- 'Songs of Womanhood', nos. 1, 3, 4; 1911;-'God is our Hope'; 1941;- 'Clown's Congé'; 1948.

51007. Five Celtic Love Songs; 1910.

51008. Smaller works for voice and chamber accompaniment: Two Duets ... arranged from folk songs; 1918;-Symbol Songs; 1920;-'Song of Lyonesse', 'Evensong'; 1923;-Five Songs; 1931;-Five Songs; 1944.

51009. Songs for voice and piano: 'The Midnight Wind'; 1895;-'Thou and I'; 1895;-'The Fox'; 1896;-'Presentiment'; 1897;-Four Faery Songs; 1901–2;-Three Baby Songs; 1902;-'May and Death'; 1902.

51010. Songs of the English; 1901.

51011. Songs for voice and piano: 'Love at Sea'; 1907;-'Sweet Evenings', 'Joy is Fleet', and 'A Sight in Camp'; 1908?;- 'The Wind'; 1916;-'Into the Twilight'; 1917;-'Apollo'; 1919;-Four Everyman Songs; 1922;- 'A Song of Cider'; 1930;-Faery Song from 'The Immortal Hour'; 1931 arrangement;-'Eros' 1931;-Bridal Song; 1932;-'The Faery People'; 1940;-'The Street'; 1940.

51012. Unaccompanied songs: 'The Devon Maid'; 1906?;-'The Wind'; 1909;-'The Dreamers'; 1924;-'Playing Shepherds'; 1924.

Presented by A. R. Boughton, Esq., and Joy Boughton, son and daughter of the composer.

51014. GIROLAMO CRESCENTINI (1766–1846): two Italian arias, with five anonymous arias; early 19th cent.

51015. WILLIAM SHIELD: three string trios; late 18th–early 19th cent.

51016–19. WILLIAM RUSSELL (1777–1814), organist, pianist and composer: musical manuscripts. As follows:

51016–18. Vocal music, mainly overtures and songs from burlettas and pantomimes; 1799–1808. Mostly *autograph.*

51019. Organ arrangements of excerpts from oratorios by Handel; 18th cent. *copy* owned by William Russell, 23 April 1792.

1963

51020. MISCELLANEOUS VOLUME:

E. Jean de Reszke: letter to ——; n.d.

M. Stefan Zweig: letter and postcard to Emily Anderson; n.d., 1938.

Presented by Alexander Hyatt King, Esq.

51023 A–C. FRANK WHITAKER: papers relating to a projected book on Béla Bartók; 20th cent.

Presented by Mrs. Hilda Whitaker, widow of the compiler.

51056–65. HAVERGAL BRIAN: *autograph* scores and sketches. As follows:

51056. Symphony no. 5, 'Siegeslied', a setting of Psalm 68 for double chorus, soprano solo and orchestra; 1933. Vocal score.

51057. Symphony no. 6, 'Wine of Summer', for solo voice and orchestra; 1937. Sketches in vocal score.

51058. Symphonia Tragica, 'Deirdre of the Sorrows'; 21 Feb. 1948. Full score.

51059. Symphony no. 7. Sketches, 1948, and full score, n.d.

51060. Symphony no. 8; 17 May 1949. Full score.

51061. Symphony no. 9; July–November 1951. Full score.

51062. Symphony no. 10; 16 Jan. 1954. Full score.

51063. Symphony no. 11; 29 April 1954. Full score.

51064. Symphony no. 12; Feb. 1957. Full score.

51065. Symphony no. 13; Nov.–Dec. 1959. Full score.

Presented by the composer.

51066–70. DOHNÁNYI SUPPLEMENTARY COLLECTION:

51066. Piano concerto in E minor, fourth movement (*autograph* fragment), and photographs, mainly of Dohnányi.

51067. Concert programmes; 20th cent.

51068. Press cuttings; 20th cent.

51069. Two letters, 1901, n.d., postcard, 1888, photographs and press cuttings, 19th–20th cent.

51070. Marion Ursula Rueth, *The Tallahassee Years of Ernst von Dohnányi*, 1962 (thesis for Master of Arts degree at Florida State University).

Add. 51066–8 presented by Mme. Kovács, sister of the composer; Add. 51069 presented by Dr. Imre Podhradszky of Budapest.

51317A–D. RALPH VAUGHAN WILLIAMS: A London Symphony; *circ.* 1914–15. Full score compiled by the composer, with the assistance of George Butterworth, Geoffrey Toye and Edward Dent, from the orchestral parts, to replace the original score lost in Germany in 1914.

Presented by Sir Adrian Boult.

52256–7. EDWARD CLARK, composer and conductor, of the B.B.C.: letters addressed to him from musicians including:

52256. Ansermet, Yvonne Arnaud, Bartók, Bax, Berg, Berkeley, Lord

Berners, Bliss, Boughton, Frank Bridge, Britten, Casella, Coates, Dalla-piccola, Darnton, Delius, Dent, Van Dieren, Edwin Evans, Falla, Fricker, Gerhard, Harty, Heseltine, Hindemith, Ireland, Kodály, Kolisch, Křenek, Kussevitsky.

52257. Lambert, Leibowitz, Milhaud, Moeran, Newman, Nin, Poulenc, Prokofiev, Schoenberg, Smyth, Sorabji, Steuermann, Stravinsky, Szigeti, Tippet, Turina, Veress, Vogel, Walton, Webern, Vaughan Williams, H. Wood.

52287. RALPH VAUGHAN WILLIAMS: Hymn Tune Prelude on 'Song 13' by Orlando Gibbons, for piano; [1928]. *Autograph*.

Presented by Miss Harriet Cohen, C.B.E.

52288–9. RALPH VAUGHAN WILLIAMS: film music for 'Scott of the Antarctic', 1948–9, and 'The Loves of Joanna Godden', 1947. Partly *autograph*.

Presented by Mrs. Ursula Vaughan Williams.

52290. RALPH VAUGHAN WILLIAMS: string quartet no. 2 in A minor; [1942–4]. *Autograph* parts.

Presented by Miss Jean Stewart (Mrs. Hadley).

52291. UNIDENTIFIED MASS; 19th cent.

Presented by K. S. Taylor, Esq.

1964

52311. MISCELLANEOUS VOLUME:
G. Franz Liszt: visiting card, with *autograph* note; n.d.

Presented by W. L. Jennings, Esq.

52334–58. AYRTON COLLECTION. Papers relating to William Ayrton (1777–1858), Musical Director of the King's Theatre and Editor of *The Harmonicon*, and to other members of the Ayrton family. The musical part of the collection is as follows:

52334. Notes by Ayrton for his projected Dictionary of Music.

52335–6. Correspondence and papers relating to the King's Theatre, including letters of Dragonetti, P. Spagnoletti, the singers, M. Kelly, J. Braham, G. Naldi, Mme Camporese, etc.

52337A. Letters of musicians including Meyerbeer, Clementi, Shield, Mendelssohn, etc.

52337B. Letter of Beethoven to Baron Pasqualati.

52344. Ayrton's account book; 1804.

52345. Papers relating to the Singing and Dancing Club, 1799.

52346. Papers relating to the Coronation Festival, 1838, of which Ayrton was musical director.

52347. Papers, including programmes, relating mainly to the Beethoven Quartet Society; 1845, etc.

Presented by Miss Phyllis Ayrton.

52363. HARPSICHORD PIECES by H. Purcell, Blow, Croft, Clarke, Dieupart, John Barrett, Weldon, Courteville, R. King, Forcer, 'Baptist' (i.e. G. B. Draghi?), John White, Francis Pigott; late 17th cent. Owned by Elizabeth Barrett in 1704.

52364–6. RUTLAND BOUGHTON: letters to him from musicians, writers, politicians, etc.; 20th cent. The musicians included are:

52364. F. Austin, Bantock, Barbirolli, Bax, Beecham, Bliss, Clara Butt, Walford Davies, Dent, T. Dunhill, Elgar, Fellowes, Kathleen Ferrier, Leon and Eugène Goossens, Holst, Järnefelt, C. Kennedy-Fraser, Fuller Maitland, Newman, P. Robeson, Landon Ronald,

52365. Letters from George Bernard Shaw, many relating to music.

52366. M. Shaw, Ethel Smyth, H. Wood.

52383. RALPH VAUGHAN WILLIAMS: film music for 'Bitter Springs'; *circ.* 1950. Partly *autograph* and partly in the hand of Ernest Irving.

Presented by Stanley Black, Esq.

52384. SIR WILLIAM WALTON: two early compositions, 'Tell me where is fancy bred' for soprano, tenor, violins and piano, and Choral Prelude on 'Wheatley' for organ; 1916. *Autograph.*

Presented by Dr. Howard Ferguson.

52385. RALPH VAUGHAN WILLIAMS: 'The Lark Ascending'; 1921. *Autograph* arrangement for violin and piano.

Presented by Miss Pauline Baring.

52421. JOHN DAVEY: collection of Cornish Carols (words only); 1795.
Repaired with the aid of a grant from the Ralph Vaughan Williams Trust.

52425. JULES MASSENET: song, 'Première Danse'; 1899. *Autograph*. With a *printed* copy, Heugel et Cie., 1899.

52426. SIR FREDERIC H. COWEN: unidentified comedy opera (characters: Lys, Pierre, Tom, Paul, Lucette, Pierrot, Pierrette, etc.); 1921. Full score. *Autograph*.
Presented by Cecil Bernard Oldman, Esq., C.B.; C.V.O.

52464A. MISCELLANEOUS MUSIC:
A (1). William Jackson of Masham: song 'Tears, Idle Tears'; 1849. *Autograph*.
(2). Renaldo Hahn: song, 'The Fallen Oak'; 1898. *Autograph*.
B (1). Alan Bush: 'Cradle Song' and 'Beauty Dwells Uncertain'; n.d. *Autograph*.
(2). Inglis Gundry: Entry Song and Bow Song from 'The Return of Odysseus'; *circ.* 1938. *Autograph*.
Presented by Alexis W. Eastwood, Esq.
C. Settings of Robert Graves's poem, 'Counting the Beats', by Lennox Berkeley, Nicholas Maw and Humphrey Searle; 1963. *Autograph*.
Presented by the Poetry Book Society.

52523. PETER WARLOCK: Early Elizabethan Songs for voice and string quartet, i.e. Warlock's transcriptions of Farrant's 'Abradad' (score and parts); Edwardes's 'When May is in his prime' (parts); N. Strogers's 'A doleful deadly pang' (score); 20th cent.

52525–35. SIR EDWARD ELGAR: *autograph* compositions. As follows:
52525. 'Rosemary'; 1882. Full score.
52526. May Song; 1901. Piano score.
52527. 'Carissima'; 1913. Full score, with 'Récit D'Amour' in vocal score.
52528. 'Polonia', op. 76; 1915. Full score.
52529. 'Une voix dans le désert', op. 77; 1915. Piano score.
52530. 'The Starlight Express', op. 78; 1915. Full score.
52531. 'Fight for the Right'; 1916. Vocal score.
52532. 'Le Drapeau Belge', op. 79; 1917. Piano and full scores.
52533. 'The Sanguine Fan', op. 81; 1917. Full score.
52534. 'The Prince of Sleep'; 1925. Vocal score.
52535. 'Beau Brummel'; 1928. Full score.
Presented by Messrs. Elkin & Co., Ltd.

52536. SAMUEL HOLMES: 'O Salutaris Hostia' and Requiem Mass in the style of Palestrina; 19th cent.

Presented by Cecil Hopkinson, Esq.

1965

52540. MISCELLANEOUS VOLUME:

    G. Aria for soprano and keyboard, beginning 'Va crescendo il grave affanno', with a note of presentation from Natale Corri to Miss Barbara Seton; 18th cent.

Presented by Edward Croft-Murray, Esq.

    J. Dr. Charles Burney: letter to Thomas Pennant mentioning the crwth, pibgorn, bagpipes, etc.; 4 Jan. 1774.

    M. Paul von Klenau: two songs including the *autograph* of 'The First Rose'; 1920, n.d.

Presented by Ernest Warburton, Esq.

52547–9. FREDERICK DELIUS: letters to Peter Warlock (Philip Heseltine), 1911–29, and (52549) letters of Mrs. Jelka Delius, mainly to Warlock, 1913–30.

Sotheby's sale 16 Dec. 1964, lot 395.

52588–90. BALLET SCORES from the collection of Harold Rubin intended for performance at the Arts Theatre:

    52588. Roberto Gerhard: 'Alegrías'; *circ.* 1941. *Autograph.*

    52589. Franz Reizenstein: Ballet Suite for small orchestra; 1940. Piano score. *Autograph.*

    52590. Edmund Rubbra: 'Prism'; 1938. *Autograph.*

52601. RALPH VAUGHAN WILLIAMS: 'O clap your Hands'; 1920. Full score. *Autograph.*

Presented by Messrs. Stainer & Bell, Ltd.

52603–7. RICHARD SIMPSON: songs. *Autograph.* As follows:

    52603–5. Settings of Shakespeare Sonnets; 1860–66.

    52606–7. Miscellaneous songs; before 1875.

Transferred from the Department of Printed Books (Music Room).

52614. RALPH VAUGHAN WILLIAMS: Three Vocalises for soprano and clarinet; 1958. *Autograph.*

52620. RALPH VAUGHAN WILLIAMS: songs and motets: 'Lord Thou hast been our Refuge', motet for chorus, semi-chorus and orchestra; 1921;-'O vos omnes', motet for mixed voices with alto solo; 1922;-'It was a Lover', part-song for two voices, with piano; 1922;-'Ca' the Yowes', arranged for tenor solo and mixed chorus; 1922;-'Darest thou now, O soul', unison song with piano or string accompaniment; 1925;- 'Magnificat' and 'Nunc Dimittis', set for the use of village choirs, for mixed chorus and organ; 1925. *Autograph.*

Presented by Mrs. Ursula Vaughan Williams.

52622. FRANZ JOSEPH HAYDN: the 'Ox' Minuet; early 19th cent. Orchestral parts.

Transferred from the Department of Printed Books (Music Room).

52871–901. THE NORAH KIRBY COLLECTION of *autograph* musical compositions by John Ireland. As follows:

ORCHESTRAL WORKS

52871. Concertino Pastorale for string orchestra; 1939. Full score.

52872. A Downland Suite for brass band, 1933. Condensed score, together with the Minuet and Elegy from the suite arranged for string orchestra [1941], in full score.

52873. 'The Forgotten Rite', 1913. Full score and piano-duet arrangement.

52874. 'Mai Dun'; 1920–1. Full score and piano-duet arrangement.

52875. Poem for orchestra; 1904. Full score.

52876. 'Satyricon', overture; 1946. Full score.

52877. 'Tritons', symphonic poem; n.d. Full score. With a condensed score of 'A Maritime Overture' [1944] arranged from 'Tritons' for military band.

52878. Piano concerto; 1930. Full score.

52879. Legend for piano and orchestra; 1933. Full score and arrangement for two pianos.

INCIDENTAL AND FILM MUSIC

52880. Incidental music for a broadcast production of 'Julius Caesar'; 1942. Full score.

52881. Music for the film, 'The Overlanders'; 1946–7. Full score.

CHAMBER MUSIC

52882. Sextet for clarinet, horn and string quartet; n.d. Full score.

52883. String quartet, no. 1, in D minor; 1897. Score.

52884. String quartet, no. 2, in C minor; 1897. Score and parts.

52885. Piano trio, no. 2, in E; 1917. Score.

52886. Piano trio, no. 3, in E; 1938. Score and *printed* proofs.

52887. Trio for clarinet, 'cello and piano; 1912–14. Score.

52888. Sonata for 'cello and piano; 1923.

PIANO SOLOS

52889. Piano pieces: 'Ballade of London Nights'; n.d.;-'Columbine'; 1949, 1951;-'The Darkened Valley'; 1921;-'Decorations'; 1912;-'Equinox'; *circ.* 1923;-'Greenways'; 1937;-'In Those Days'; 1895 revised 1941;-'Intruder' (rewritten as 'Cypress'); n.d.;-'London Pieces'; 1917, 1920.

52890. Piano pieces: Meditation on John Keble's Rogationtide Hymn for organ; 1958;-'Month's Mind'; 1933;-'On a Birthday Morning'; 1922;-Prelude in E flat; 1924;-Preludes('Obsession' only); 1915;-First Rhapsody; 1906;-'Sarnia'; 1940–1;-'Sea Idyll'; 1900;-'Soliloquy'; 1922.

52891. Piano pieces: Sonata; 1918–20;-'Three Pastels'; 1941;-'The Towing Path'; 1918;-Two Pieces, 'For Remembrance', 'Amberley Wild Brooks'; 1921;-Two Pieces, 'April', 'Bergomask'; 1925;-Two Pieces, 'February's Child', 'Aubade'; 1929, 1930;-'Vilanella' (organ and piano versions), 1911, 1912.

VOCAL WORKS

52892. 'These Things shall be', for baritone solo, chorus and orchestra; 1937. Sketches, and full score in the hand of Alan Bush.

52893. Psalm 42 for soli, chorus and string orchestra; 1908. Full score.

52894. 'Ex Ore Innocentium' for treble voices with organ or piano; 1944;-'Magnificat' and 'Nunc Dimittis'; n.d.;-'Te Deum' in C; 1941;-'Vexilla Regis' for chorus, soli, trumpets, trombones and organ; 1898. Full score.

52895. Part-songs: 'Cupid'; n.d.;-'Laughing Song'; 1910;-A New Year Carol; 1941;-'The Peaceful Western Wind'; n.d.

52896. Unison songs: 'The Boy'; n.d., published 1942;-'Boy's Names'; 1941;-'O Happy Land'; 1941;-'Ride a Cock-Horse'; 1941.

52897. Songs: 'Annabel Lea', recitation with piano; *circ.* 1910;-Five Poems by Thomas Hardy; 1926;-Five 16th cent. Poems; 1938;-'A Garrison Churchyard'; 1916;-'Great Things'; 1925;-'Here's to the Ships'; 1912;-'The Holy Boy'; n.d.

52898. Songs: 'If we must part'; 1929;-'The Land of Lost Content';
1920–1;-'Love is a Sickness'; 1921;-'Marigold'; 1913;-'Santa Chiara';
circ. 1924;-Songs of a Wayfarer; 1911;-Songs Sacred and Profane;
1929, 1931.

52899. Songs: Three Songs, 'The Adoration', 'The Rat', 'Rest'; 1918,
1919;-Three Songs, 'Love and Friendship', 'Friendship in Misfortune',
'The One Hope'; 1926;-Two Songs, 'My True Love', 'The Trellis';
1920;-'Vagabond'; 1922;-'We'll to the Woods no more'; 1927;-'What
art thou thinking of'; 1924;-'When I am dead, my dearest'; 1924.

SKETCHES

52900. Miscellaneous.

52901. Sketchbooks.

Presented by Mrs. Norah Kathleen Kirby.

52904–12. PETER WARLOCK: *autograph* music manuscripts; 1917–1930. As
follows:

52904. 'A Chinese Ballet'; 1917. Piano score.

52905. 'Kano Kernow': settings of two Cornish carols for four unaccompanied voices; 1918.

52906. 'Saudades': three songs, with a cancelled setting of 'The Water
Lily'; 1916–17.

52907. Seven songs, 'The Passionate Shepherd', 'The Contented Lover',
'Youth', 'The Sweet O' the Year', 'Tom Tyler', 'Elore Lo', 'The Droll
Lover'; 1928.

52908. 'Corpus Christi', for soprano and baritone with string quartet;
circ. 1923. Score and parts.

52909. Six songs, 'The Fairest May', 'My Lady is a Pretty One', 'Sleep',
'Take, Oh take those Lips away', 'Chopcherry', 'My ghostly Fader',
for solo voice and string quartet; in a music-book dated 1918–30.
Score.

52910. Two songs, 'A Sad Song' and 'Pretty Ring-Time', for soprano
and small orchestra; *circ.* 1922, 1925. Score and parts.

52911. 'Maltworms' for baritone solo, male voice chorus and orchestra;
1926. Full score.

52912. Smaller works: 'The Old Codger' (piano arrangement of themes
from César Franck's Symphony in D minor), 1916; 'The Cloths of
Heaven', 1919; 'The Curlew' (for tenor, flute, cor anglais and string

quartet, in condensed score, imperfect), 1920–2; 'Jenny Gray', n.d.; 'Queen Anne' and 'Row well, ye Mariners', 1928.

Sotheby's sale 20 July 1965, lots 409, 410, 412, 413, 424; together with lots 422; 415; 417 (most), 419, 423; 408, 414, 418 purchased from Messrs. Quaritch, H. Baron, Esq., Richard Mancutt, Esq., and Messrs. Blackwell respectively.

52915. GUSTAV HOLST: six songs (settings of poems by Humbert Wolfe), and 'Dawn' from Hymns from the Rig Veda; 1929, 1907–8. *Autograph.*

Presented by Miss Vally Lasker.

52917. SCHIFF PAPERS. This volume includes letters to Sydney Schiff from Frederick and Jelka Delius; 1921–32.

Presented by Mrs. Freda Gardner through the Hon. Julian Fane.

52927. RICHARD STRAUSS: two pages of draft of 'Capriccio', not included in the final version; *circ.* 1940–1. *Autograph.*

Presented by Mrs. Mignon Aber.

1966

53709. MISCELLANEOUS VOLUME:

C. Dr. [Edward?] Hodges: overture for organ; 1824. Possibly *autograph.*

Presented by Dr. Alan Tyson.

I.   Sir Arnold Bax: letter to Philip Heseltine; n.d.
Richard Macnutt, Catalogue 98, no. 7.

53717–20. NORMAN O'NEILL: incidental music. Mostly *autograph.* As follows:

53717. 'The Blue Bird'; 1909. *Autograph* full score and cued *printed* text.

53718. 'Julius Caesar'; 1920. *Autograph* full score and cued *printed* text.

53719. 'Mary Rose'; 1920. Full score (*copy* with *autograph* annotations).

53720. 'The Merchant of Venice'; 1922. *Autograph* full score and cued *printed* text.

Presented by Mrs. Yvonne Hudson, daughter of the composer.

53721–2. WILLIAM H. HENLEY: unaccompanied studies for the violin and (53722) transcriptions of eight works for violin and piano by Heinrich Wilhelm Ernst, the 19th century virtuoso, including his Polonaise de Concert, op. 17; 20th cent. *Autograph.*

Presented by Sydney Twinn, Esq.

53723. HENRY LAWES: volume containing 325 songs and dialogues; before 1630–after 1650. *Autograph.*

53734. SIR CHARLES VILLIERS STANFORD: two fugues, à 3 and 4, for piano, and two pieces, 'Ballata' and 'Ballabile', op. 160, for 'cello and piano; 1922, 1923; 1928. *Autograph.*

Presented by Dr. Howard Ferguson.

53735. SIR ARNOLD BAX: 'Moy Mell' for two pianos; 1916. *Autograph.*

Presented by Dr. Howard Ferguson.

53739–66. DENIS APIVOR: *autograph* compositions; 20th cent. As follows:

OPERAS AND BALLETS

53739A, B. 'She stoops to Conquer', op. 12.

53740–1. 'Le Menagier de Paris', ballet, op. 18; 1951. Piano score and full score.

53742–3. 'A Mirror for Witches', ballet, op. 19; 1951. Piano score and full score.

53744. 'Saudades', ballet, op. 27; 1955. Piano score.

CHORAL WORKS

53745–6. 'Thamar and Amnon', op. 25; 1954. Vocal score and full score.

53747. Cantata, op. 32; 1960–1. Full score.

53748. 'The Secret Sea', op. 38; 1964. Full score (the vocal score is in the Library of the University of Texas).

53749. Early songs, mainly op. 3 but including part of opp. 1, 2 and 6; 1935–9.

53750. Four songs of Thomas Lovell Beddoes, op. 24; 1953.

ORCHESTRAL WORKS

53751. Nocturne on a song of Diego Pisador, op. 4; 1938. Full score (string orchestra).

53752. 'Bouvard and Pecuchet', overture, op. 17; 1950. Full score.

53753–4. Symphony, no. 1, op. 22; 1952. Study score and full score.

53755. 'Overtones', op. 33; 1961. Full score.

53756. Symphony, no. 2, op. 36; 1963. Full score.

CONCERTOS

53757. Concertante for clarinet and orchestra with percussion, celesta and harp, op. 7a; 1958 (revised from the 1945 version). Full score.

53758. Concerto for piano and orchestra, op. 13; 1948. Two-piano score.

53759. Concerto for violin, op. 16; 1950. Study score.

CHAMBER WORKS

53760. Wind quintet, op. 31; 1960.

53761. 'Mutations', op. 34, for 'cello and piano; 1962.

53762. String quartet, op. 37; 1964.

53763. 'Crystals', op. 39, sextet for Hammond Organ, guitar, double bass, marimba and two percussion players; 1964.

SOLO INSTRUMENTAL WORKS

53764. Variations for solo guitar, op. 29; 1958.

53765. Piano pieces, op. 30; 1960.

53766. 'Animalcules', op. 35, twelve pieces for piano solo; 1963.

Mostly presented by Denis ApIvor, Esq.

53767–70. HOLLANDER COLLECTION: letters to the Dutch violinist, conductor and composer, Benno Hollander (1853–1942), including letters of Saint-Saëns, and Hollander's draft memoirs (53769–70); 19th–20th cent.

53771. SIR MICHAEL TIPPETT: 'Midsummer Marriage'; [1952–54]. Full score. *Autograph.*

53777–9. SIR ARTHUR SULLIVAN: *autograph* full scores of 'Patience' (53777) and 'The Gondoliers' (53779), with a copyist's full score of 'Patience' (53778); *circ.* 1881, 1889, etc.

Purchased at Sotheby's sale 13 June 1966, lots 183, 186, with contributions from the Arts Council, The Pilgrim Trust, the Wates Foundation, the Gilbert and Sullivan Society, the Friends of the National Libraries and the appeal organized by the D'Oyly Carte Opera Trust.

1967

54177. GEORGE HART: catalogue of musical literature collected by him; 1903. *Presented by Messrs. Sotheby & Co.*

54186–91. RALPH VAUGHAN WILLIAMS: *autograph* music manuscripts; 1878–early 19th cent. As follows:

54186. 'The Robin's Nest'; 1878.

54187–91. Folksong collections; early 19th cent.

Presented by Mrs. Ursula Vaughan Williams.

54193. FRANCIS EDWARD BACHE (1833–58): letters to his parents describing his musical studies in London and Leipzig, etc., with other papers; *circ.* 1840–53.

Hodgson's sale 31 *March* 1967, *lot* 512.

54194. WILLIAM WORDSWORTH: his music-book containing copies of songs by Arne, Handel, John Eccles, H. Purcell and Blow, sonatas by Abel, etc.; 18th cent.

Hodgson's sale 31 *March* 1967, *lot* 512.

54197. PETER WARLOCK (Philip Heseltine): letters to Colin Taylor; 1911–29.

Presented by Colin Taylor, Esq.

54207. ROBERTO VALENTINI: six sonatas for two violoncelli; early 18th cent.

54208–10. ROGER QUILTER: incidental music for the children's fairy play, 'Where the Rainbow Ends', etc.; *circ.* 1911, etc. As follows:

54208. Full score.

54209. Notebook of dances; 1934.

54210. Libretto. *Typewritten.*

Presented by Miss Ruth Conti.

54212–3. HAVERGAL BRIAN: Symphony no. 27, 1966, and Sinfonia in C minor, 1967. Full scores. *Autograph.*

Presented by the composer.

54214. RALPH VAUGHAN WILLIAMS: Nine English Folksongs from the Southern Appalachian Mountains, with piano accompaniments by Vaughan Williams; *circ.* 1939. *Autograph.*

Presented by Mrs. Ursula Vaughan Williams.

EGERTON MANUSCRIPTS
of music acquired 1910–1966

Eg. 2888. MUSIC TREATISES: (1) Prologue begins 'Quoniam discretorum industria', text begins 'Principio disserenti de musica';-(2) Prologue begins 'Primum tractatum huius uoluminis', text begins 'Animaduertendum est quia quod Boetius tropos'; 2nd half of 12th cent.

Eg. 2910–46. GRANVILLE COLLECTION. Works by George Frideric Handel, mostly in the hand of John Christopher Smith, senior. Scores. The manuscripts belonged to Bernard Granville (1709–75) of Calwich Abbey, co. Stafford. The dates given are mostly those of composition. As follows:

Eg. 2910–13. Eleven of the Chandos Anthems, 1716–20, with the Funeral Anthem, 1727, in place of [Arnold's] no. 12.

Eg. 2914. The Utrecht 'Te Deum' and 'Jubilate', 1713; Chandos 'Te Deum' in B flat, *circ.* 1718–20; 'Te Deum' in D, *circ.* 1714.

Eg. 2915–30. Operas:

Eg. 2915. 'Rinaldo'; 1711, with 1731 songs.

Eg. 2916. 'Teseo'; 1712.

Eg. 2917. 'Amadis'; 1715.

Eg. 2918. 'Ottone'; 1722.

Eg. 2919. 'Il Giulio Cesare'; 1723.

Eg. 2920. 'Tamerlane'; 1724.

Eg. 2921. 'Rodelinda'; 1725.

Eg. 2922. 'Scipio'; 1726, with 1730 additions.

Eg. 2923. 'Alessandro'; ended April 1726.

Eg. 2924. 'Admetus'; end of 1726.

Eg. 2925. 'Richard'; 1727.

Eg. 2926. 'Siroe'; 1728.

Eg. 2927. 'Lothario'; 1729.

Eg. 2928. 'Ariodante'; 1734.

Eg. 2929. 'Imeneo'; 1738–40.

Eg. 2930. 'Deidamia'; 1740.

Eg. 2931–9. Oratorios:

Eg. 2931. 'Esther'; 1720, with 1732 additions.

Eg. 2932. 'Deborah'; ended Feb. 1733.

Eg. 2933. 'Athaliah'; June 1733.

Eg. 2934. 'Il Trionfo del Tempo'; *circ.* 1737.

Eg. 2935. 'Saul'; July–Sept. 1738.

Eg. 2936. 'Israel in Egypt'; Oct. 1738.

Eg. 2937. 'The Messiah'; Aug.–Sept. 1741.

Eg. 2938. 'Samson'; Sept.–Oct. 1741.

Eg. 2939. 'Joseph'; 1743.

Eg. 2940. 'Acis and Galatea'; *circ.* 1720.

Eg. 2941. 'L'Allegro, Il Penseroso, ed Il Moderato', 1740, preceded (ff. 1–10b) by the Concerto Grosso, op. 6, no. 10.

Eg. 2942. Fifty Italian cantatas.

Eg. 2943. Twelve Italian duets, 1710–12, and a trio, 1708.

Eg. 2944. Twelve Concerti Grossi, op. 6; 1739.

Eg. 2945. Eleven organ concertos; 1735–43.

Eg. 2946. The Water Music, 1715–16; Concerto for two violins and 'cello, with orchestra, 1736.

Eg. 2953. GEORGE FRIDERIC HANDEL: 'Acige e Galatea', cantata incorporating part of the English Pastoral, 'Acis and Galatea'; 18th cent. Mostly in the hand of John Christopher Smith, senior; a few words are in Handel's *autograph* and four leaves (ff. 98–101b), dated 1708, are *autograph* and derive from the manuscript (now British Museum R.M. 20. a. 2) of the original version of the work.

The following manuscripts, Eg. 2954–71, were acquired at the sale of William Hayman Cummings's library, Sotheby's 17–24 May 1917.

Eg. 2954. MUSIC TREATISES: (1) 'Tractatus super musicam mensuratam magistri Johannis de Muris';-(2) 'Regule utiles super contrapuncto', apparently by a pupil of J. de Muris; 15th cent.

Eg. 2955. FELIX MENDELSSOHN BARTHOLDY: Scherzo, Notturno and Wedding March from 'A Midsummer Night's Dream', arranged for piano; 1844. *Autograph.*

Eg. 2956. HENRY PURCELL: 'The Yorkshire Feast Song'; *circ.* 1689. Full score. *Autograph.*

Eg. 2957. RICHARD LEVERIDGE: music in 'Macbeth'; late 17th cent. At ff. 14–18 is an alternative version of 'Now I go'.

Eg. 2958. HENRY PURCELL: song, 'I came, I saw and was undone'; 17th–18th cent.

Eg. 2959. HARPSICHORD AND ORGAN PIECES by Croft, Blow, Froberger, H. Purcell, Robert? King; 17th–18th cent.

Eg. 2960. ANTHEMS, DUETS, SONGS, by Carissimi, Sances, Casati, Reggio, Aldrich, H. Purcell, Blow, Courteville, R. Ramsey, Humfrey, Locke, C. Gibbons, Captain Cook?; late 17th cent. Partly in the hand of Henry Bowman.

Eg. 2961–2. ITALIAN SONGS, with a bass for harpsichord, by Sabbatini, Severo da Lucca, Bononcini, Giovanni del Violone, Pollarolo (in Eg. 2961), Pasquini, A. Scarlatti, Mancia [F. Mancini?] (in Eg. 2962); late 17th cent. Owned by Henriette Scott, 'her book from Rome, 1697' (note in each volume).

Eg. 2963. JEAN BAPTISTE LULLY: 'Alceste'; late 17th cent. Full score.

Eg. 2964. DR. WILLIAM BOYCE: anthem, 'The souls of the righteous'; late 18th cent. Full score.

Eg. 2965. DR. WILLIAM CROFT: anthem, 'Rejoice in the Lord'; 17th–18th cent. Full score. *Autograph.*

Eg. 2966–8. STRING QUARTETS by G. Paisiello and Wenzel Pichl and a Serenata by the latter for clarinet, violin and viola; late 18th cent. Parts (lacking the 'cello part).

Eg. 2969. HENRY PURCELL: Ode for St. Cecilia's Day; 18th–19th cent. Full score, apparently in the hand of John Saville, lay-chorister of Lichfield Cathedral.

Eg. 2970. HARPSICHORD SOLOS, mainly arrangements of popular tunes, songs, etc., by Hasse, C. J. Stanley, Handel, Sullivan, William? Felton, Martini, S. Howard; 18th cent.

Eg. 2971. ENGLISH AND ITALIAN SONGS, with accompaniments for harpsichord or bass viol, by R. Jones, N. Giles, Coperario, D. Farrant; early 17th cent.

Eg. 3002, f. 2b. MADRIGAL, 'In willdernys ther fond I Bes', for 3 voices in quasi-score; early 16th cent.? (Found with a courtbook in the Heath and Verney Papers.)

Eg. 3009. MISCELLANEOUS VOLUME:

    D. Dr. Charles Burney: letter to —— relating to the authorship of 'God Save the King'; 29 July 1806. With further notes by Burney and Sir Joseph Banks.

    E. George Frideric Handel: inventory of his household effects valued at £48 and sold by order of the executor to Handel's servant, John Du Bourk; 27 August 1759.

Eg. 3019. FRANCESCO BASILI, Maestro di Capella at the Vatican: Mass in A minor; 19th cent. *Autograph*.

Eg. 3022–4. ANTONIO OTTOBONI: opera, 'Proserpina Rapita'; 18th cent. Full score.

Eg. 3040. FRÉDÉRIC CHOPIN: two polonaises, op. 40, no. 1 in A and no. 2 in C minor; 1838–9. *Autograph*.

Eg. 3042. EDVARD GRIEG: 'Foran sydens Kloster', op. 20, for soprano, alto and women's chorus: *circ.* 1871. Full score. *Autograph*.

Eg. 3051. COLLECTION OF FROTTOLE, STRAMBOTTI AND ODES, with music for four voices by Italian composers of the 15th and early 16th century including F. d'Ana, B. Tromboncino, M. Cara, F. de Luprano, N. Brocus, G. Fogliani, Josquin des Prés; *circ.* 1500.

Eg. 3087. ALEKSANDR PORFIREVICH BORODIN: draft of the 'Petite Suite' for piano, with a draft of the Scherzo in A flat for piano; 1885. *Autograph*.

Eg. 3090–7. FREDERICK GEORGE EDWARDS, Editor of *The Musical Times*: correspondence and papers; 1877–1909. As follows:

    Eg. 3090. Letters from Elgar, Parry and Stanford.

    Eg. 3091. Letters from Sir George Grove.

    Eg. 3092. Letters from Sir J. Stainer, E. J. Hopkins, J. A. Fuller-Maitland.

    Eg. 3093. Letters from J. S. Bumpus, W. Cowan.

Eg. 3094. Letters and papers relating to Mendelssohn and to Edwards's *History of Mendelssohn's Elijah*, 1896, including letters of Mendelssohn's daughter, Mrs. Marie Benecke, and Miss Elizabeth Mounsey.

Eg. 3095–6. Miscellaneous letters of musicians including S. Coleridge-Taylor, Walford Davies, Sir E. German, Otto Goldschmidt, Joachim, Jenny Lind, MacDowell, Niecks, Prout, Richter, H. Watson.

Eg. 3097A. Miscellaneous papers including proofs of articles on Niecks and Elgar with their *autograph* corrections; an *autograph* extract by Elgar from one of the 'Quadrilles for an Eccentric Orchestra'; *autograph* part-song by Elgar; *autograph* fragment of Granville Bantock; chants, including *autographs* of W. G. Alcock and J. H. Maunder.

Eg. 3097B. Miscellaneous: including a fragment of a letter of Beethoven to Nanette Streicher [1818]; hair of Weber, Samuel Wesley, S. S. Wesley, and Mendelssohn; leaves from the graves of Mozart, Beethoven and Schubert at Vienna; photographs of S. S. Wesley, Verdi, Sterndale Bennett, and Moscheles.

Eg. 3146. GIUSEPPE SCARLATTI, opera, 'La Clemenza di Tito'; before 1760. Full score. *Autograph.*

Eg. 3158. HUGO WOLF: letters to Professor Carl and Frau Rosa Mayreder; 1895–8. *German.*

Eg. 3159. WOLF AND BRUCKNER: (1) two letters of Hugo Wolf to Dr. Oskar Grohe and Dr. Heinrich Potpeschnigg; 1890, 1899;-(2) letter of Anton Bruckner to Richard Batka; 1894. *German.*

Eg. 3246. TCHAIKOVSKY AND RICHARD STRAUSS: (1) letter of Petr Ilich Tchaikovsky to Frau Marie von Bülow; 1888. *French*;-(2) Letters of Richard Strauss to Edward Speyer; 1899–1925. *German.*

Eg. 3250. RICHARD STRAUSS: song, 'Ständchen', op. 17, no. 2; 1886. *Autograph.*

Eg. 3251. RALPH VAUGHAN WILLIAMS: Concerto Academico for violin and string orchestra; 1924–5. Full score. *Autograph.*

Eg. 3288–9. SPANISH SONGS, with a few Portuguese and Italian songs, with accompaniments for piano or guitar; before 1819. As follows:

Eg. 3288. Songs by F. Moretti, M. Rücker, J. F. Acuña, P. del Moral, Beramendi, and anonymous.

Eg. 3289. Songs by Beramendi, F. Maximo, T. de Yriarte, F. Moretti, V. Fioravanti, F. Sors, and anonymous.

Eg. 3290. JOHN DAVY: incidental music to 'Rob Roy', 'Harlequin Quick-silver', 'Miller's Maid'; 1818, 1804, 1804. Full scores. *Autograph*. With a *copy* of a Pas de Deux by Auber.

Eg. 3301–6. PERCY PITT PAPERS. Correspondence of Percy Pitt (d. 1932), musical director at Covent Garden, etc.; 1892–1932. As follows:

Eg. 3301–2. Letters from Hans Richter, with some from Pitt to Richter; 1903–14. German.

Eg. 3303. Correspondence with Elgar; 1899–1932.

Eg. 3304–6. Letters to Pitt, mainly from musicians, including Ansermet, Melba, F. Austin, Bantock, Beecham, Boughton, Busoni, Charpentier, Cowen, Dale, Debussy, Delius, Baron d'Erlanger, German, E. Goossens, Henschel, Holst, Mackenzie, Messager, Parry, Puccini, Ravel, Saint-Saëns, C. Scott, Dame Ethel Smyth, R. Strauss, Siegfried Wagner, W. Wallace, Vaughan Williams, E. Wolf-Ferrari, H. Wood.

Eg. 3307. WINDSOR CAROL-BOOK: polyphonic music consisting of liturgical music for Holy Week and Eastertide, thirty-three carols, drinking song and a motet, probably written for St. George's Chapel, Windsor; between 1430–44.

Eg. 3512. THOMAS TALLIS: forty-part motet, 'Spem in alium non habui', with English words, 'Sing and glorifie'; *circ.* 1610–16? Full score.

Eg. 3664. THOMAS CLAYTON: opera, 'Arsinoe'; early 18th cent. Full score.

Eg. 3665. THE TREGIAN MANUSCRIPT: madrigals, motets, fancies, etc., copied by Francis Tregian (d. 1619) mainly from printed sources (some no longer extant) including works by F. Anerio, Caccini, Coperario, Dering, Du Caurroy, M. East, Alfonso Ferrabosco, senior and junior, Gesualdo, T. Lupo, Marenzio, Monteverdi, Morley, Pallavicino, Ward and many other composers; before 1619. Score.

Eg. 3666. J. S. BACH: 'Die Kunst der Fuge'; 18th–19th century. Copy owned by Johannes Brahms.

Eg. 3669–70. SIGFRIED KARG-ELERT (d. 1932); Partita in E for organ, op. 100, and letters to Godfrey Sceats; 1924, 1922–31. *Autograph*.

Eg. 3685–8. JOHANN CHRISTIAN BACH: recitatives and arias from operas; 18th cent. As follows:

Eg. 3685. 'Temistocle'.

Eg. 3686. 'Catone in Utica'.

Eg. 3687. 'Alessandro nel'Indie'.

Eg. 3688. 'Artaserse'.

Eg. 3722. WILLIAM BYRD: *autograph* certificate on behalf of Dorothy Tempest; 1581.

Sotheby's sale 11 Oct. 1954, lot 60.

Eg. 3767. TREBLE PART-BOOK of anthems and services by H. Purcell, Blow, Croft, J. Clarke, T. Kelway and V. Richardson; early 18th cent.

Eg. 3768. WILLIAM DAVIS of Worcester: anthem, 'Let God arise'; 1709. *Autograph.*

Eg. 3770. SIR ARTHUR BLISS: ballet, 'Checkmate'; 1937. Full score. *Autograph.*

Eg. 3771. SIR WILLIAM WALTON: Polka from 'Façade'; 1922. Draft score. *Autograph.*

Eg. 3778. JOSEPH RITSON: *Ancient Songs,* 1790. *Printed,* with manuscript annotations.

MUSIC MANUSCRIPTS ON LOAN
to the Department of Manuscripts

LOAN 4. ROYAL PHILHARMONIC SOCIETY. Music manuscripts. As follows:

LUDWIG VAN BEETHOVEN

RPS. MS. 21. Ninth Symphony, op. 125; [1824]. Full score. *Copy* with *autograph* corrections.

RPS. MS. 518. 'Kleine Ouverture zu den Ruinen von Athen', op. 113; 1815. Full score. *Copy* with *autograph* annotations.

RPS. MS. 519. 'Namensfeier' Overture, op. 115; 1815. Full score. *Copy* with *autograph* corrections.

RPS. MS. 520. Overture to 'König Stephan', op. 117; 1815. Full score. *Copy* with *autograph* annotations.

RPS. MS. 521. Overture, 'Die Weihe des Hauses', op. 124; 1822. Full score. *Copy* with *autograph* corrections.

SIR WILLIAM STERNDALE BENNETT

RPS. Supplement 4. 'Parisina', 'Naiades', 'Wood Nymphs'; 1835. Full scores. Partly sketches. *Autograph.*

LUIGI CHERUBINI

RPS. MS. 40. Symphony in D; 1815. Full score. *Autograph.*

RPS. MS. 582. Overture in G; 1815. Full score. *Autograph.*

JOHANN BAPTIST CRAMER

RPS. MS. 1021. Quintet for piano and strings in B flat; 1832. Full score. *Autograph.*

FRANÇOIS FÉMY

RPS. MS. 90. Symphony in E minor; *circ.* 1816. Full score. *Autograph.*

FRANZ JOSEPH HAYDN

RPS. MS. 136. Symphony no. 98 in B flat; (no. 4 of the first set of Salomon symphonies); *circ.* 1792. Full score. *Copy* with a few bars possibly in the composer's *autograph.*

RPS. MS. 137. Symphony no. 95 in C minor (no. 5 of the Salomon symphonies); 1791. Full score. *Autograph.*

RPS. MS. 138. Symphony no. 96 in D (no. 6 of the Salomon symphonies); 1791. Full score. *Autograph.*

HEINRICH KARL JOHANN HOFMANN

RPS. MS. 217. 'Frithjof', op. 22; *circ.* 1874. *Printed* full score with an *autograph* letter.

FELIX MENDELSSOHN BARTHOLDY

RPS. MS. 289. Symphony in C minor, no. 1, op. 11; 1824, etc. Full score. *Autograph.*

RPS. MS. 777. Trumpet Overture in C, op. 101; before 1833. Full score, with separate *autograph* trombone parts.

RPS. MS. 779. Overture, 'Fair Melusina', op. 32; *circ.* 1833. Full score. *Copy* with *autograph* corrections.

IGNAZ MOSCHELES

RPS. MS. 1194. Septet for clarinet, horn, strings and piano, op. 88; 1833. Full score. *Autograph.*

THEA MUSGRAVE

RPS. Supplement 10. Clarinet concerto; 1968. Full score. *Photostat copy.*

SIGISMUND VON NEUKOMM

RPS. MS. 804. Fantasy for orchestra; 1806. Full score. *Autograph.*

IGNAZ JOSEPH PLEYEL

RPS. MS. 367. Symphony in C; *circ.* 1800. Full score. *Autograph.*

RPS. MS. 368. Symphony in E flat; *circ.* 1801. Full score. *Autograph.*

RPS. MS. 369. Symphony in A minor; n.d. Full score. *Autograph.*

RPS. MS. 370. Symphony in B flat; n.d. Full score. *Autograph.*

CIPRIANI POTTER

RPS. MS. 374. Symphony in G minor; 1832. Full score. *Autograph.*

RPS. MS. 375. Symphony in C minor; 1834. Full score. *Autograph.*

RPS. MS. 376. Symphony in D; 1834. Full score. *Autograph.*

RPS. MS. 377. Symphony in B flat, with the Allegro con fuoco from the Symphony in G minor (see RPS. MS 378); 1821, 1819. Full score. *Autograph.*

RPS. MS. 378. Symphony in G minor; before 1826. Full score. *Autograph.*

RPS. MS. 379. Symphony in D; 1833. Full score. *Autograph.*

RPS. MS. 837, 837*. Overture in E minor, original and revised versions; 1815, 1848. Full scores. *Autograph.*

RPS. MS. 838. Overture, 'Cymbeline'; 1836. Full score. *Autograph.*

RPS. MS. 839. Overture, 'Antony and Cleopatra'; 1835. Full score. *Autograph.*

RPS. MS. 840. Overture, 'The Tempest'; 1837. Full score. *Autograph.*

RPS. MS. 1216. Piano concerto in E; 1835. Full score. *Autograph.*

RPS. MS. 1217. Piano concerto in E flat; *circ.* 1833. Full score. *Autograph.*

RPS. MS. 1218. Piano concerto in D minor; 1832. Full score. *Autograph.*

ANTON JOSEPH REICHA

RPS. MS. 854. Overture in E; n.d. Full score. *Autograph.*

DAME ETHEL SMYTH

RPS. Supplement 2. Two interlinked French folk melodies for small orchestra; n.d. Full score. *Autograph.*

LUDWIG SPOHR

RPS. MS. 922. Overture in F; before 1821. Full score with a separate trombone score. *Autograph.*

RICHARD STRAUSS

RPS. Supplement 5. Overture, 'Macbeth', op. 23; 1936. First page only, in full score. *Autograph.*

GERMAINE TAILLEFERRE

RPS. Supplement 9. 'Cantate du Narcisse'; n.d. Vocal parts. *Copies* with *autograph* annotations.

JOSEPH VLACH VRUTICKÝ

RPS. Supplement 1. 'Prologue Symphonique de la Tragédie', for orchestra; 20th cent. Full score. *Autograph?*

CARL MARIA VON WEBER

RPS. MS. 961. 'Jubel-Ouverture'; 1818. Full score. *Copy* with *autograph* title.

FELIX WEINGARTNER

RPS. Supplement 3. Sinfonietta for string trio and orchestra, op. 83; n.d. Full score. *Autograph.*

RALPH VAUGHAN WILLIAMS

RPS. Supplement 6. Sinfonia Antartica; *circ.* 1949–52. Full score. *Autograph.*

Lent by the Royal Philharmonic Society, 1914, with subsequent additions.

LOAN 13. SIR EDWARD ELGAR. Symphony in A flat, op. 55, Enigma Variations, op. 36, 'The Apostles', op. 49, Violin Concerto, op. 61, and Piano Quintet in A minor, op. 84. Full scores. *Autograph.*

Lent by Mrs. Carice Elgar Blake, daughter of the composer, 1934.

LOAN 17. SIR EDWARD ELGAR. *Autograph* sketches for his unfinished Third Symphony; 1933.

Lent by the British Broadcasting Corporation, 1935. Presented to the Museum by the British Broadcasting Corporation in 1969 and numbered Add. MS. 56101.

LOAN 29, Vol. 333. PORTLAND PAPERS. A volume of miscellaneous fragments including the following items of music:

1. A single paper leaf containing 'All þof I can' (Cantus part) and 'O v[ost]re rotte' (Contratenor and Tenor parts); added in a different hand are the Tenor and Bassus? parts of a textless piece, and the Treble part of 'Mari'; late 15th cent. ff. 70, 70b.

2. An unnumbered vellum fragment containg the Treble part of 'Adoro te Domine'; early 16th cent.

3. An unnumbered vellum fragment containing ornamental cadences; early 15th cent.

From the collection of papers lent by His Grace the Duke of Portland. K.G., 1947, with subsequent additions.

LOAN 42. WOLFGANG AMADEUS MOZART. *Autograph* music manuscripts. As follows:

1. Mozart's own thematic catalogue of his compositions from Feb. 1784 to Nov. 1791.

2. Mozart's marriage contract; 3 Aug. 1782. *Signed.*

3. Four letters to his cousin, Anna Thekla Mozart, 5 Nov. 1777, 28 Feb. 1778, 23 Dec. 1778, 10 May 1779; one letter to Professor Anton Klein, 21 May 1785.

4. 'Das Veilchen', K. 476.

5. String quintet in E flat, K. 614.

6. Quintet for armonica, flute, oboe, viola and 'cello, K. 617.

7. Concerto for horn and orchestra, K. 447.

8. Cherubino's aria, 'Non sò più', from 'The Marriage of Figaro', K 492.

9. Last movement of the string quartet in D minor, K. 173.

10. March in C major for orchestra, K. 408, no. 1.

11. Five Contredances, K. 609.

12. Canons, K. 559, 560a.

13. Sonata for piano and violin, K. 377.

14. Duettino from 'La Clemenza di Tito', K. 621, no. 3.

15. Former covers, sale-catalogues, etc.

Lent by the heirs of Stefan Zweig, 1957.

LOAN 44. SIR EDWARD ELGAR. *Autograph* music manuscripts. As follows:

1. Bound volume containing 'Salut d'amour', op. 12 (sketch); 'My love dwelt in a Northern Land', no. 8; 'Liebesahnung' (sketch) and other fragments.

2. 'The Shepherd's Song', op. 16, no. 1.

3. Bound volume containing 'Through the long Days and Years', op. 16, no. 2; 'Queen Mary's song', no. 9; 'The Poet's Life', no. 10; 'Is she not passing fair', no. 32.
4. Serenade for strings, op. 20. Score for two pianos.
5. 'From the Bavarian Highlands', op. 27.
6. Organ Sonata, op. 28.
7. 'Te Deum' and 'Benedictus', op. 34. Full score.
8. 'Te Deum' and 'Benedictus' (rough sketches).
9. Enigma Variations, op. 36. Sketches.
10. Enigma Variations, op. 36. One sheet of score of the Coda.
11. 'Sea Pictures', op. 37. Full score.
12. Pomp and Circumstance March, op. 39, no. 1. Full score.
13. Pomp and Circumstance March, op. 39, no. 4. Full score.
14. Cockaigne Overture, op. 40. Full score.
15. Cockaigne Overture, op. 40. Sketches.
16. 'Speak Music', and 'In the Dawn', op.41, nos. 1 and 2.
17. 'Dream Children', op. 43.
18. Introduction and Allegro, op. 47. Full score.
19. Bound volume containing 'Pleading', op. 48; 'Arabian Serenade', no. 40; 'Chariots', no. 41.
20. 'The Reveille', op. 54. Vocal score.
21. Song cycle, op. 59, nos. 3, 5, 6.
22. 'The Torch', op. 60, no. 1. Full score.
23. 'The River', op. 60, no. 2. Full score.
24. Violin concerto, op. 61. Piano score.
25. Romance for bassoon and orchestra, op. 62.
26. 'Great is the Lord', op. 67. Full score.
27. 'Sospiri', op. 70. Full score.
28. 'Carillon', op. 75. Full score.
29. 'The Fourth of August', op. 80, no. 1. Full score.
30. 'To Women', op. 80, no. 2.
31. 'For the Fallen', op. 80, no. 3. Full score.
32. 'With proud Thanksgiving', arranged from 'For the Fallen', op. 80, no. 3. Full score.
33. Transcription of the Fugue in C minor by Bach, op. 86. Full score.
34. Another copy of 33.
35. Severn Suite, op. 87. Sketches.
36. Bound volume containing 'Ecce sacerdos magnus', no. 6; 'Sospiri', op. 70.
37. 'My Love dwelt in a Northern Land', no. 8.
38. Serenade Lyrique, no. 17. Full score.
39. 'To the Queen', no. 18. Vocal score.

40. 'Evening Scene', no. 30. Vocal score. Sketches.
41. 'The Birthright', no. 42. Sketches.
42. 'The Wanderer', no. 51.
43. 'Remember', no. 52. Vocal score.
44. 'King Arthur', no. 53. Sketches.
45. 'Carillon Loughborough', no. 54.
46. Hymn on the Nativity, no. 61.
47. 'Good Morrow', no. 62. Vocal score.
48. 'Mina', no. 72. Full score.
49. Hymn tune, 'Darwell', orchestrated by Elgar. Full score.

Lent by Mrs. Carice Elgar Blake, daughter of the composer, 1958.

LOAN 48. ROYAL PHILHARMONIC SOCIETY. Papers, correspondence, etc. As follows:

1. Foundation Book; 1813.
2. Directors' Minute Books; 1816–1908. Twelve volumes.
3. General Minute Books; 1813–1918. Three volumes.
4. Rough Minute Books; 1871–96. Four volumes.
5. Miscellaneous official papers.
6. Letter books containing *copies* of letters from the Royal Philharmonic Society; 1831–76. Five volumes.
7. Recommendations for associateship and membership with signatures of the applicants.
8. Subscribers' Lists; 1813–68 *passim. Printed.*
9. Finance. Account books, 1813–79, balance sheets, 1866–88, receipts (mainly from performers), orchestra lists and takings, 1908–10, etc.
10. Press cuttings.
11. Catalogues of music belonging to the Society and of music performed.
12. *Printed* music with manuscript annotations: Elgar, *Variations for Orchestra*, op. 36; Handel, *Solomon*, copy used by Sir Thomas Beecham.
13. Letters of musicians addressed to the Society, arranged in alphabetical order, including Beethoven, Berlioz, Brahms, Debussy, Delius, Dvořák, Elgar, Grieg, Holst, Liszt, Mendelssohn, Sibelius, R. Strauss, Tchaikovsky, Vaughan Williams, Wagner; 19th–20th cent. Thirty-seven volumes.
14. Material relating to Beethoven, including a lock of his hair, half a laurel leaf from a wreath thrown onto his grave, miscellaneous papers including *copies* of letters to and from Beethoven, papers relating to financial assistance given to Beethoven with letters of Moscheles, *copy* of the canon, 'Es muss sein', documents relating to Mme Fanny Linzbauer's gift to the Society of the Schaller bust of Beethoven, etc., miscellaneous *printed* pamphlets, reports relating to Beethoven, two

copies of J. M. Levien, *Beethoven and the Royal Philharmonic Society*, 1927, *photograph* of a letter from Beethoven to Moscheles, 18 March 1827 (in Schindler's hand), with a list of metronome markings relating to the Ninth Symphony.

15. Miscellaneous: newspapers and magazines relating to the Society; photographs; ivory counters admitting Directors, etc., to concerts; conductor's baton.

16. Catalogue of the Society's papers compiled by Myles Birket Foster. Two volumes.

Lent by the Royal Philharmonic Society, 1961.

LOAN 49. RICHARD STRAUSS AND ZOLTÁN KODÁLY. Music manuscripts as follows (the Strauss manuscripts are *autograph*; the Kodály are mostly *copies*):

STRAUSS

1. String quartet, op. 2. Score.
2. Five Piano Pieces, op. 3.
3. Withdrawn.
4. Violin concerto, op. 8. Piano score.
5. Symphony, op. 12. Full score.
6. Piano quartet, op. 13. Score.
7. 'Wanderers Sturmlied', op. 14. Full score.
8. Songs, op. 19.
9. Songs, op. 21.
10. Songs, op. 29.
11. Songs, op. 32.
12. Songs, op. 36.

KODÁLY

13. 'Méditation' for piano.
14. Two folksongs from the Zobor district. Score.
15. Two songs op. 5. Full score.
16. Seven songs, op. 6.
17. Five songs, op. 9.
18. Second string quartet, op. 10. Score.
19. Three songs, op. 14.
20. Ballet Music. Full score.
21. Marosszék Dances. Piano score.
22. 'Pange Lingua'. Score.
23. Dances of Galánta. Full score.
24–28. Hungarian folksongs, vols. 6–10.

Lent by Universal Edition (London) Ltd., 1961.

LOAN 53. SIR ARNOLD BAX. *Autograph* music manuscripts. As follows:

1. First Symphony; 8 Oct. 1922. Full score.
2. Second Symphony; March 1926. Full score.
3. Third Symphony; Feb. 1929. Full score.
4. Fifth Symphony; Dec. 1931–March 1932. Full score.
5. Sixth Symphony; *circ.* 1934. Piano score. Incomplete.
6. Concerto for 'cello and orchestra; 19 Dec. 1932. Full score.
7. Violin concerto; March 1938. Full score.
8. 'Enchanted Summer' ('Prometheus Unbound'); Dec. 1910. Full score.
9. 'Christmas Eve'; 1911. Full score.
10. 'Christmas Eve'; Jan. 1912. Full score.
11. Symphonic Scherzo; 1917 revised 1933. Full score.
12. Romantic Overture for small orchestra; [1923?]. Piano score.
13. Romantic Overture for chamber orchestra; April 1926. Full score.
14. 'The Tale the Pine Trees knew'; Dec. 1931. Full score.
15. Prelude for a Solemn Occasion; Feb. 1933. Full score.
16. Nonett; Jan. 1930. Full score.
17. Quintet for piano and strings; 16 July 1914–13 Apr. 1915. Score.
18. Withdrawn.
19. Quartet in one movement; summer 1922. Score.
20. Second string quartet; 5 Feb. 1925. Score.
21. Third string quartet; 23 Sept. 1936. Score.
22. Piano trio in B flat; 9 Jan. 1946. Score.
23. Second sonata for violin and piano; 1915.
24. Third sonata for violin and piano; [1927].
25. Sonata in F for violin and piano; Sept. 1928.
26. Withdrawn.
27. Withdrawn.
28. Withdrawn.
29. Withdrawn.
30. A Rabelaisian Catechism, 'La Foi d'la loi'; 16 Aug. 1920.
31. Withdrawn.
32. 'I heard a soldier'; 31 March 1924.
33. 'Eternity'; 6 Sept. 1925.
34. 'Walsinghame'; May 1926.

Lent by the late Miss Harriet Cohen, C.B.E., 1964. These manuscripts have been bequeathed to the Museum and renumbered in the series Additional MSS. 54724–81.

LOAN 54. FREDERICK DELIUS. Music manuscripts, mainly *autograph*. As follows

1. Five piano pieces: Mazurka, two waltzes, Toccata, Lullaby; 1891–1923, n.d. In the hand of Mrs. Delius.

2. 'Fennimore and Gerda'; 1909–10. Full score. *Autograph.*

3. 'An Arabesk'; 1911. Full score. *Autograph.*

4. Requiem; 1914. Full score. *Autograph.*

5. Concerto for 'cello and orchestra; 1921. Full score. *Copy* in the hand of C. W. Orr.

Lent by Universal Edition (London) Ltd., 1964.

LOAN 56. SIR ARNOLD BAX, SIR EDWARD ELGAR AND JOHN IRELAND. Music manuscripts. *Autograph* unless otherwise stated. As follows:

BAX MANUSCRIPTS

1. First Symphony; 1921. Piano score.

2. Second Symphony; 1924. Piano score.

3. Third Symphony; *circ.* 1929. Piano score.

4. Symphonic Variations for piano and orchestra; 1917. Piano score, with a separate variation in full score, and a *copy* of the full score.

5. 'Winter Legends' for piano and orchestra; 1929. Two-piano score and *copy.*

6. Movement headed 'III' 'Allegro' for piano and orchestra; n.d. Piano score.

7. Concertino for piano and orchestra; [1939]. Condensed score. *Draft.*

8. Concertante for piano, left-hand ;[1949]. Piano score.

9. Phantasy for viola and orchestra; [1920]. Full score.

10. 'The Well of Tears' for voice and orchestra; 1914. Full score.

11. 'Eternity' for voice and orchestra; 1934. Full score.

12. Pageant of St. George for voice and orchestra (with other unidentified sketches, including Prelude, Allegretto, Gavotte); n.d.

13. 'November Woods'; 1917. Piano score.

14. 'The Truth about the Russian Dancers' for orchestra; 1920. Full score.

15. First and Third Northern Ballads for orchestra; 1927. Piano scores.

16. 'Winter Legends'; 1930. Full score.

17. 'The Tale the Pine Trees knew'; 2 Oct. 1931. Piano score.

18. Saga Fragment for orchestra; after 1922. Full score. *Copy.*

19. Sonata in E for violin and piano; 1910. The Finale is a *copy.*

20. Sonata in E for violin and piano (second and third movements) different from the preceding sonata; March 1925.

21. 'In the Night', passacaglia for piano; 1914.

22. Piano sonata in F; 1913.

23. 'Ideala' for piano; 1916.

24. Second piano sonata; 1919.

25. Third piano sonata in G sharp minor; 1926.

26. Piano sonata in B flat, 'Salzburg'; n.d.

27. Suite on the name Gabriel Fauré for piano; 1945. *Copy.*

28. Summer Music; *circ.* 1920. Piano score.

29. Romanza and Phantasie for piano; 1947.

30. Three Rondels by Chaucer; 1914. For voice and piano.

31. 'The Song of the Dagger', from 'The Bard of the Dimbovitza'; *circ.* 1914.

32. 'My eyes for Beauty pine', song; n.d.

33. Songs, vol. I; 1905–10.

34. Three Songs from the Norse; 1927. *Copy* (the *autograph* is in the University Library, Copenhagen).

OTHER COMPOSERS

35. Sir Edward Elgar: (1) *Autograph* cadenza from his unfinished piano concerto; *circ.* 1933;-(2) Two-piano arrangement by Dr. Percy Young of the Poco Andante, the second movement of the piano concerto; 1955. Two *copies*.

36. John Ireland: Legend for piano and orchestra; *circ.* 1933. Piano score (*copy*), with a leaf of *autograph* corrections.

37. Withdrawn.

SUPPLEMENT

38. Sir Arnold Bax: 'Spinning song', from 'The Bard of the Dimbovitza'; 1914.

Lent by the late Miss Harriet Cohen, C.B.E., 1964. These manuscripts have been bequeathed to the Museum and renumbered in the series Additional MSS. 54724–81.

LOAN 59. SIR MICHAEL TIPPETT. Opera, 'King Priam'; 1961. Full score. *Autograph.*

Lent by Karl Hawker, Esq., 1966.

Note: The collection of manuscript music belonging to the Royal College of Music, formerly Loan 28, was returned to the College in 1961.

MUSIC MANUSCRIPTS
IN THE MUSIC ROOM
Department of Printed Books

The following manuscripts are available to holders of Readers' tickets through the Reading Room.

THE ROYAL MUSIC LIBRARY

A collection of printed and manuscript music deposited on loan in the British Museum by King George V in 1911 and presented to the Museum by Queen Elizabeth II in 1957. The collection is described in: *Catalogue of the King's Music Library*, Part I (The Handel Manuscripts), by W. Barclay Squire, 1927, Part II (The Miscellaneous Manuscripts), by Hilda Andrews, 1929, Part III (Printed Music and Musical Literature), by William C. Smith, 1929. The contents of this catalogue are not repeated here, except for certain manuscript items inserted in printed volumes. Two volumes of anthems by Handel, in the hand of an amanuensis, apparently strays from the Royal Collection, were placed on loan by Messrs. Novello & Co., Ltd. in 1958, and purchased from them in 1970. They are numbered R.M. 19.g.1a and 1b. The following Handel manuscript was omitted from the printed catalogue:

> R.M. 19 f. 10. 'Arianna'; mid 18th cent. Score, comprising the songs only, without the recitatives and instrumental numbers.

CHAPEL ROYAL MANUSCRIPTS

Part-books of anthems, services, etc.; 17th–19th cent. Deposited on loan in 1927, and presented in 1958 for inclusion in the Royal Music Library. Five additional volumes were presented in 1968. As follows:

> R.M. 23. m. 1–6. Six volumes. For this set see H. Watkins Shaw, 'A contemporary source of English music for the Purcellian period', *Acta Musicologica*, 1959, fasc. 1, pp. 38–44.
>
> R.M. 27. a. 1, etc. Ninety volumes, and a manuscript index. A card index of the contents of these volumes is in the Music Room.

MISCELLANEOUS MUSIC MANUSCRIPTS

These consist of manuscript music acquired with printed collections, or bound with or entered in single printed volumes, and a few items preserved in the general library. Items already described in A. Hughes-Hughes, *Catalogue of Manuscript Music in the British Museum*, 1906–9, are excluded.

ABBEY GLEE CLUB, founded 1841. A collection of printed and manuscript volumes (E. 205, E. 205. a–q, H. 1202, H. 1202. a–z) presented in 1959. The manuscript items are as follows:

E. 205. p, q. Miscellaneous collection of glees.

H. 1202. jj. Attendance register; 1887–1905.

H. 1202. kk. Index of glees in the collection.

H. 1202. ll. Record of performances of glees, etc.; 1895–1929.

JOHANN KASPAR AIBLINGER

Hirsch III. 595. Cantata, 'Jesu, mein Ein und Alles'; *circ.* 1840.

ANTHEMS

K. 7. e. 2. Single parts of anthems bound with J. Barnard, *The First Book of selected Church Music*, 1641, as follows: in the Tenor cantoris part, anthems by A. Bryne, O. Gibbons, G. Marson, T. Tomkins, T. Wilkinson and anonymous; in the Bassus decani part, anthems by H. Aldrich, R. Alison, A. Batten, W. Byrd, W. Cranford, J. Foster, C. Gibbons, O. Gibbons, R. Hutchinson, H. Lawes, M. Peerson, Thomas Preston of Durham, A. Shaw, T. Tallis, T. Tomkins, T. Wanless, T. Wilkinson, M. Wise and anonymous; 17th–early 18th cent.

G. 970. Four anonymous anthems. Bound with T. Williams, *Harmonia Coelestis*, 1780.

DANIEL FRANÇOIS ESPRIT AUBER

K.6.e.2. 28 bars of a textless duet for soprano and tenor with pianoforte accompaniment; dated 'Juillet 1852'. *Autograph.* In papers relating to *The Wandering Minstrels*, vol. 2, f. 80v.

CARL PHILIPP EMANUEL BACH

K. 10. a. 28. Manuscript variants added to Sonatas 3–5 in *VI Sonates pour clavecin avec des reprises variées*, 1760. *Autograph.*

BÉNIGNE DE BACILLY

K. 1. d. 25. *Les Airs spirituels sur les stances chrétiennes de Monsieur l'Abbé Testu*, 1672, 77. With manuscript alterations and nine leaves of additional songs in manuscript, apparently intended for an enlarged edition. Possibly *autograph*.

ADÈLE BALMANI-NALDI

Hirsch III. 627. Recitative and aria; *circ.* 1820. Full score.

ANTON FRANZ BECZWARZOWSKY

R.M. 15. a. 13. Letter to the Prince of Wales; 1813.

LUDWIG VAN BEETHOVEN

Hirsch M. 1345. Violin concerto, op. 61, arranged for violin and piano; mid 19th cent.

Hirsch 5121. Aloys Fuchs: 'Notizen über Ludwig v. Beethoven'; 1851–52.

Hirsch 2324. Programm des dritten Konzertes des Beethoven-Bundes; 1904.

VINCENZO BELLINI

Hirsch II. 46. 'La Sonnambula'; mid 19th cent. Full score.

Hirsch M. 1346. Scena, 'Vedi, o madre', from 'La Sonnambula'; 1829.

ORAZIO BENEVOLI

Hirsch IV. 692. 'Messa a 16 voci'; early 19th cent.

L. BOCCHERINI

h. 42. n. *Concerto IV per il violoncello obligato, circ.* 1780. *Printed* parts, with full score and piano reduction in the hand of Adam Carse.

ERCOLE BOTTRIGARI

Hirsch 5234. a. 'Il Desiderio'; 1594. German translation by Kathi Meyer, published 1924.

MONSIEUR BOUTH?

Hirsch M. 1347. Valse anglaise; *circ.* 1842.

SIR JOHN FREDERICK BRIDGE

R.M. 14. c. 21. Letter to Sir H. F. Ponsonby; 1887.

ROBERT BROADLEY

H. 1501. (3.) Song, 'If thoul't be mine'; 1849.

OLIVIA DUSSEK BUCKLEY

R.M. 8. f. 16. (1.) Letter to Queen Victoria; 1845.

JOHN SKELTON BUMPUS

G. 518. a–c. A collection of printed and manuscript church music in three volumes, chiefly by English composers, compiled, annotated and partly transcribed by J. S. Bumpus, with an index to each volume. Including *autograph* music by H. H. Pierson, Sir F. A. G. Ouseley, and other nineteenth-century church musicians.

WILLIAM BYRD

K.2.f.1. A setting, apparently by Byrd, of 'What pleasures have great princes' entered in contemporary manuscript on sig. Bii of each part of his *Psalmes, sonets & songs,* 1588, except the Bassus.

CATALOGUES

Hirsch IV. 1081. Gottfried Dunwalt: 'Catalogus musicalium Godefridi

Dunwalt Canonici Collegiatae Ecclesiae B. Mariae V. ad Gradus Coloniae'; 1770.

Hirsch IV. 1075. Munich: 'Catalogus librorum musicorum, tum manuscriptorum, tum impressorum, in Electorati Bibliotheca Bavarica Monacensi asservatorum'; early 19th cent.

Hirsch IV. 1085. Comte d'Ogny: 'Catalogue de la musique de Monsieur le Comte d'Ogny'; late 18th cent.

Hirsch IV. 1068. Various collections:

Breslau: 'Concept des Catalogs über die auf der Universitätsbibliothek zu Breslau befindliche, alte Musik', by C. von Winterfeld; 1819.

Cassel: 'Auszug aus dem Musikalien Verzeichniss des Museums zu Cassel'; early 19th cent.

Heinrichau: two lists of music, including the collection at the Stiftskirche, by C. von Winterfeld; 1811.

Liegnitz: 'Musikbücher auf den Ritterakadamien zu Liegnitz', by C. von Winterfeld; early 19th cent.

Munich: 'Register über die Musiksammlung aus dem 16 und 17 Jahrhundert, welche in der Hofbibl. zu München aufbewahrt wird' by J. N. Forkel; 18th cent.

Neisse: 'Verzeichniss der im Kreuzh: Stifte zu Neisse vorgefundenen musikal: Kirchenstücken' [sic]; 1811.

CATCH CLUB. See below: Noblemen's and Gentlemen's Catch Club.

CATCHES

K. 1. e. 9, 10. Catches by W. Cranford, J. Hilton, and E. Nelham; early 17th cent. Written in copies of T. Ravenscroft, *Pammelia*, 1609, and *Deuteromelia*, 1609.

P. CAVALLO

Hirsch IV. 1455. Autograph album, 1845–53, containing pieces or musical quotations by F. W. Kücken, J. B. Cramer, I. Moscheles, G. Preyer, J. B. Stiegler, L. Batta, A. Batta, B. Cossmann, L. Le Cieux, A. H. Chelard, A. L. Clapisson, A. P. F. Boëly, C. V. Alkan, G. A. Osborne, F. Hünten, L. Niedermeyer, D. Alard, F. Bonoldi, A. Leemann, L. Dorus, A. Quidant, A. Ropicquet, S. Verroust, J. P. Pixis, T. Pixis, F. Godefroid, T. Döhler, F. Servais, A. A. Klengel, G. A. Petter, F. Wartel, J. Blumenthal, H. de Montour, W. Kruger, A. Lefébure-Wély, T. Boehm, L. Séjan, V. Blancou, F. Viret, M. Mayer, H. Wohlers, A. Guillot, C. Fradel, E. Wolff, J. Rosenhain, L. Müller, E. Arnaud, C. Haas, P. Moralt, H. P. Seligmann, O. Comettant, P. Henrion, J. Meifred, R. Wagner, J. van der Heyden, F. C. David, C. Oberthür.

F. T. A. CHALUZ DE VERNEVIL

R.M. 14. a. 21. Letter to Queen Victoria; 1849.

MONTAGUE CORRI
R.M. 13. e. 3. Letter to William IV.

GIULIO COTTRAU
G. 691. c. (20.) 'Marcia Sinfonica'; *circ.* 1883. Full score.
G. 691. c. (22.) 'Marcia Sinfonica'; 1878. Full score.
G. 691. c. (23.) 'Serenata spagnuola per soprano'; n.d. Score. *Autograph.*
G. 691. c. (24.) Quartetto, no. 3.; *circ.* 1880. Score.
G. 691. c. (24*.) Gavotte, 'La Danse des esprits'; 1888. Score. *Autograph.*
G. 691. c. (25.) 'Sinfonia dell' opera Griselda . . . Riduzione per Banda Militare'; n.d.
G. 691. b. (19.) Song, 'Tutto ritorno'; *circ.* 1910. *Imperfect draft. Autograph.*

DANCES
a. 30. a. Dances for the violin or flute with instructions for the flute; 18th cent. In *The Compleat Tutor to the Violin. The Fifth Book,* 1727.
a. 26. h. Dance tunes. In *Select Minuets,* [1729].
b. 58. c. Dance tunes, bound with *The Repository of Scots, & Irish Airs, etc.,* [1796?]

FRANZ DANZI
Hirsch IV. 1144. Opera, 'Deucalion et Pirrha'; *circ.* 1800. Vocal score.

GAETANO DONIZETTI
Hirsch II. 208. 'Belisar'; mid 19th cent. Full score. *German* words.
Hirsch II. 214. 'Don Pasquale'; 19th cent. Full score. *French* words.
Hirsch II 212. 'Linda di Chamouny'; mid 19th cent. Full score. *German* words.
Hirsch II. 213. 'Lucia di Lammermoor'; mid 19th cent. Full score. *Italian* and *German* words.
Hirsch M. 1346. Scena and duetto, 'Pria di lasciarti', from 'Lucia di Lammermoor'; 1829.

HON. JOHN GREY SEYMOUR EGERTON
K. 6. e. 4. Overture, 'Endymion'; 1862. Full score. *Autograph.*

SIR GEORGE JOB ELVEY
R.M. 14. d. 7. Letter; 1839.

FRANCESCO FEDERICI
Hirsch III. 742. Scena and duetto, 'Ma dimmi, deh taci', etc., from 'La Zaira'; *circ.* 1810.

FRIEDRICH VON FLOTOW
Hirsch II. 232. 'Alessandro Stradella'; 19th cent. Full score.
Hirsch II. 231. (2.) 'Martha'; 19th cent. Incomplete full score. *French* words.

FRANCHINO GAFORI

Hirsch IV. 1441. 'Theoriae Mvsicae Tractatus'; *circ.* 1480. The same work, with variants, as his *Theoricum opus musice discipline,* 1480. *Autograph.*

PIERRE GAVINIÈS

h. 210. u. (4.) Violin concerto in A; *circ.* 1800. Solo part.

FRANCESCO GEMINIANI

Hirsch III. 214. a. Concerti grossi, op. 2; 18th cent. Copied from the Walsh edition of 1732. Parts.

CHRISTOPH WILLIBALD VON GLUCK

g. 996. b. (12.) Overture to 'Iphigénie en Aulide'; *circ.* 1790. For keyboard.

Hirsch IV. 1152. 'Orpheus' (Vienna version); *circ.* 1800. Vocal score. *German* and *Italian* words.

SIR JOHN GOSS

R.M. 14. d. 14. Letter to Sir H. F. Ponsonby; 1872.

PAUL GRAENER

Hirsch IV. 1445. 'Trommellied des Landsturms'; *circ.* 1915. *Autograph.* With a drawing by Max Liebermann on the title-page, and a letter from the artist referring to it.

W. A. GREBST

Hirsch IV. 751. 'Der Blumen Verwunderung'; *circ.* 1900.

GEORGE FRIDERIC HANDEL

e. 5. w. Overtures to 'Esther' and 'Samson', 'O sleep why dost thou leave me' from 'Semele'; mid 18th cent. Bound with printed music by John Sheeles.

MORITZ HAUPTMANN

Hirsch IV. 793. 'Aus dem 143 Psalm'; 1855. *Autograph.*

SIR JOHN HAWKINS

Case 45. f. 4–8. *A General History of . . . Music,* 1776, with a letter and manuscript notes by Dr. Charles Burney.

L.R. 39. a. 6. Another copy with manuscript notes by the author.

FRANZ JOSEPH HAYDN

Hirsch IV. 1060. 'Verzeichniss von derjenigen [sic] Kompositionen, welche ich mich beyläufig erinnere von meinem 18ten bis in das 73 Jahr componirt zu haben'; 19th cent. *copy* of the Elssler catalogue of 1805.

Hirsch M. 1355. First movement of the Surprise Symphony [No. 94.], arranged for piano duet; *circ.* 1800.

PAUL HIRSCH

Hirsch 5903, etc. A large collection of papers relating to the formation of the Hirsch Library and its use up to 1946.

GUSTAV HOLST
  Hirsch M. 1348. Carol, 'Lullay my liking'; 1916. *Autograph.*

BURNHAM W. HORNER
  R.M. 9. d. 12. Letter to Queen Victoria.

HYMNS
  Case 39. d. 3. Words of hymns, with two melodies; mid 17th cent. *German.*
  Bound with *Danck-Altar,* 1644.
  A. 1411; A. 1411. m; C. 141. k, x, bb, cc; C. 142. l, o, z, ii; D. 123. e–p, s;
  F. 1124. v. A Collection of printed hymn books acquired from Messrs.
  Novello & Co., containing letters and other documents principally
  relating to copyright, and manuscript hymn tunes, mostly *autograph.*
  Including letters from: Sir W. Sterndale Bennett, J. B. Dykes and W.
  Macfarren (D. 123. e), Sir J. Stainer (D. 123. i, o); and hymns by Sir
  J. F. Bridge, M. B. Foster, J. H. Maunder and J. E. West (D. 123. f, k),
  Sir J. Barnby, Sir F. H. Cowen, Sir G. C. Martin, Sir C. H. H. Parry and
  B. Tours (D. 123. f), C. H. Lloyd (D. 123. k).

INSTRUMENTAL MUSIC
  d. 24. Seven instrumental pieces (treble and bass, or treble parts only),
  including 'Kensington Gardens', and four cebells attributed to G. Finger,
  R. King, J. B. Lully, and H. Purcell; late 17th–18th cent. Bound at the
  end of a collection of printed airs from operas.
  g. 443. f. Three pieces, the first two for piano and violin, the third for
  piano solo; early 19th cent.

JOHN JENKINS
  K. 7. c. 2. (1.) 'Mr Jenkens his 3 parts for 2 trebels and one Bass'. Cantus,
  Altus and Bass parts; *circ.* 1680.

ALBERT WILLIAM KETÉLBEY
  g. 860. (1.) Letter to H. Wild; 1928.

KONRADIN KREUTZER
  Hirsch II. 488. 'Das Nachtlager in Granada'; mid 19th cent. Full score.

MME LANFRAY CHAUFTIÈRE
  Hirsch M. 1347. Album musical; 1842.

LILIUKALANI, QUEEN OF HAWAII
  R.M. 13. f. 11. (1.) Letter to Queen Victoria; 1897.

JEAN BAPTISTE LULLY
  Hirsch III. 906. Music from 'Cadmus ed Hermione', 'Thesée', 'Carnaval
  Mascarade'; *circ.* 1700.
  Hirsch IV. 1692. a. 'Recueil des plus beaux endroits des Opéra de M^r.
  de Lulli', Tome II. With a *printed* index bearing the imprint of le Sieur
  Foucault, Paris; early 18th cent.

LUTE TABLATURE

Hirsch M. 1353. Lute tablature, including works by Anthony Holborne and Richard Alison, with anonymous items; late 16th cent.

1242. g. 1. Dance (English); late 16th–early 17th cent.

K. 3. m. 21. Anonymous lute pieces, in Michelangelo Galilei, *Il primo libro d'intauolatura di liuto*, 1620.

MAGNIFICATS

A. 339. b. Tenor part of Magnificats by O. di Lasso and M. Varotti; late 16th–early 17th cent. Bound with O. di Lasso, *Magnificat octo tonorum*, 1573.

MANDOLINE

h. 188. m. Tunes for the mandoline (French); late 18th cent. Bound with Pietro Denis, *Méthode pour apprendre à jouer de la mandoline.*

NICOLA MATTEIS

Hirsch IV. 1633. 'Arie diverse per il violino'; *circ.* 1690. With *printed* title-page, but different contents from any of the printed collections.

JOHANN SIMON MAYR

Hirsch II. 565. 'Elisa ossia il monte di S. Bernardo'; mid 19th cent. Full score.

Hirsch II. 566. 'I Misteri Eleusini'; mid 19th cent. Full score.

J. H. MEES

R.M. 12. b. 3. Letter to the Prince Regent; 1819.

FELIX MENDELSSOHN BARTHOLDY

K. 10. a. 31. (5.) Fugue in D minor by J. S. Bach [BWV 539] copied by Mendelssohn.

Hirsch M. 1349. Additional aria for 'St. Paul', 'Der du die Menschen lässest sterben', op. 112, no. 2; *circ.* 1840. Full score.

g. 708. Scherzo, from the Octet, op. 20, arranged for orchestra by the composer. On paper with watermark date 1857. Bound with a *printed* score of Symphony No. 1.

MOTETS

K. 2. b. 10. (5.) Anonymous motets, 'Filia Formosa', 'Converte Domina'. Treble part. In *Septimus Liber Modulorum*, 1556. (Superius.)

D. 32. Anonymous motets, 'Sacerdos et pontifex', 'Tota pulchra es', 'O sacrum convivium'. First Tenor part. Bound with Varotti, *Liber primus missarum*, 1595. (Cantus.)

C. 263. Anonymous motet, 'Sub tuum praesidium'; 17th cent. Alto and Bass parts in L. Leoni, *Sacri flores*, 1619, p. 17.

WOLFGANG AMADEUS MOZART

K. 6. e. 2. Studies in counterpoint, and sketch for the finale of the piano quartet, K. 493. *Autograph.* In papers relating to *The Wandering Minstrels,* vol. 2, f. 17v.

e. 490. t. Two anonymous cadenzas for the piano concerto, K. 466; 19th cent.

Hirsch M. 1350. 'Madamina', from 'Don Giovanni'. Copy of the melody of the second section with a *German* translation by Wilhelm Meckbach; 1924.

Hirsch M. 1355. 'Cinque, dieci, venti', and 'Non più andrai' from 'The Marriage of Figaro'; *circ.* 1800.

Hirsch 5641. Wilhelm Meckbach, 'Mozart's Idomeneo'; 1917.

Hirsch IV. 1449. Requiem, K. 626. Arranged for the piano in the hand of Simon Sechter.

Hirsch M. 1351. Symphony in E flat, K. 543; early 19th cent. Full score.

NADERMANN (music publisher)

Hirsch M. 1356. Letter and receipt to Birchall, Lonsdale & Mills; 1820.

GIUSEPPE NICCOLINI

Hirsch II. 687. 'Giulio Cesare nelle Gallie'; early 19th cent. Full score.

NOBLEMEN'S AND GENTLEMEN'S CATCH CLUB, founded 1761. A collection of printed and manuscript volumes (E. 1858, E. 1858. a–z, aa–dd, H. 2788, H. 2788. a–z, aa–zz, aaa–ggg) presented in 1952. The manuscript items are as follows:

E. 1858. e–z, aa, bb. Prize catches and glees for the years 1769–72, 1774–7, 1779, 1780, 1782–4, 1786–90, 1792, 1811, 1812, 1821, 1822, 1827–35.

E. 1858. cc. Glees by W. Linley.

E. 1858. dd. Volume of songs and keyboard pieces.

H. 2788. p–z, aa–ii. Twenty volumes of glees, in multiple copies.

H. 2788. jj. Volume of songs and keyboard pieces.

H. 2788. kk. General index.

H. 2788. ll, mm. Indexes to printed music.

H. 2788. nn–pp. Indexes to manuscript music.

H. 2788. qq. Laws and regulations, 1818–78.

H. 2788. rr–ww. Minutes, 1761–96, 1827–1911.

H. 2788. xx–zz, aaa. Attendances, 1791–1850.

H. 2788. bbb. Members elected, 1779–1868.

H. 2788. ccc. Pieces chosen, 1780–1803.

H. 2788. ddd, eee. Glees performed, 1828–71.

H. 2788. fff. Cash book, 1828–51.

H. 2788. ggg, hhh. Fines, 1828–36.

VINCENT NOVELLO

K. 5. b. 8. Letter to George Canning, with a *copy* of a letter to Sir Joseph Banks regarding the proper direction of the musical department of the

British Museum and offering his services as music librarian; 22 May 1824.

JACQUES OFFENBACH

Hirsch II. 691. 'Orfeus in der Unterwelt'; 19th cent. Full score.

Hirsch II. 690. 'Die schöne Helena'; 19th cent. Full score.

FERNANDO PAER

Hirsch II. 698. Scena, 'Prometeo al Caucaso', and Duetto, 'Ettore ed Andromaca'; early 19th cent. Full score.

GIOVANNI PAISIELLO

Hirsch III. 972. Quartetto, 'A voi dono il mio core'; circ. 1810. Score.

GIOVANNI BATTISTA PERGOLESI

Hirsch IV. 1241. 'Stabat Mater'; circ. 1808. Vocal score arranged by Mündersdorf.

CIRO PINSUTI

R.M. 10. a. 8. Letter to Queen Victoria.

PSALMS

A. 1231. p. Collection of psalms, the first by Bishop. Cantus part. Bound with John Bishop, A Sett of new Psalm Tunes in four Parts, third edition, circ. 1725.

B. 512. gg. Psalm settings, some unfinished; late 18th cent. Bound with J. Barwick, Harmonia cantica divina, [1783?]

HENRY PURCELL

Hirsch III. 472. Five keyboard arrangements; late 17th–early 18th cent. Bound with his Choice Collection of Lessons, 1696.

G. 970. 'Saul and the witch of Endor'. Bound with T. Williams, Harmonia Coelestis, 1780.

JEAN PHILIPPE RAMEAU

Hirsch II. 767. (2.) Selection from 'Castor et Pollux'; 18th cent. Short score.

FRANÇOIS RÉBEL

Hirsch II. 794. 'Pirame et Thisbé'; 18th cent. Full score.

FERDINAND RIES

Hirsch M. 1352. Variations sur un Air Russe (pianoforte duet), op. 14; early 19th cent.

GIOACCHINO ROSSINI

Hirsch M. 1346. Duets from 'La Donna del Lago', 'Elisabetta', 'Ricciardo e Zoraide'; 1829.

Hirsch II. 812. 'Otello'; mid 19th cent. Full score. German words.

JEAN JACQUES ROUSSEAU

Case 26. g. 8. 'Airs principaux du Devin du village', with plates A–N (as printed in his *Dictionnaire de musique*, Paris, 1768) signed 'Ch. Baron'; *circ.* 1752–68.

MAJOR RUSHFORTH

D. 596. aa. A Hymn for Easter Day; early 19th cent.

CAMILLE SAINT-SAËNS

G. 691. a. (25.) 'Cantabile dans le duo d'amour', from 'Samson et Dalilah'. In the hand of G. Cottrau.

JOHANN ADOLF SCHEIBE

Hirsch IV. 905. 'Der Tod ist verschlungen'; 1763. *Autograph.*

JOSEPH LUDWIG SCHELL

Hirsch III. 1068. 'Gesänge, mit Begleitung des Forte-piano'; 1809.

FRANZ SCHREKER

Hirsch II. 849. 'Flammen'; *circ.* 1898. Full score. *Autograph.*

EMMA MOORE SCOTT

R.M. 8. k. 13. Letter to Sir H. F. Ponsonby; 1889.

SERVICES

K. 7. e. 2. Single parts of services bound with J. Barnard, *The First Book of Selected Church Music*, 1641, as follows: in the Contratenor cantoris part, services by—Boyce, R. Farrant, W. King, R. Portman and B. Rogers; in the Bassus decani part, services by A. Bryne, N. Pattrick, Thomas Preston of Durham and Thomas Preston junior; 17th–early 18th cent.

SONGS, etc.

A. 233. French chanson, 'Adieu nous vous verrions un jour'; 17th cent. Words only. In *De Floridi Virtuosi . . . Madrigali*, 1600. Bass part.

Hirsch III. 1116. Dialoghi a 2 voci by E. Bernabei, C. Caproli, L. Calista, A. Stradella, Vulpio; late 17th cent.

Hirsch III. 896. Collection of anonymous Italian arias, some by B. Pasquini; late 17th–early 18th cent.

K. 7. c. 23. 'Fundamenta zum Singen . . . Anno 1715', and sixteen songs, mostly sacred, in Christoph Mietzschingen, *Musicalischer Andachts-Garten*, 1690.

Hirsch III. 1012. 'Recueil de chansons'; mid 18th cent.

Hirsch III. 1014. 'Recueil de musique à chanter à voix seule'; 1755.

Hirsch III. 1010. 'Recueil d'airs tirées [sic] des meilleurs autheurs', including A. E. M. Grétry, F. A. D. Philidor; late 18th cent.

a. 76. b. (3.) Song, 'Spietato oh! Dio'; late 18th–early 19th cent. In F. T. Schumann, *A Collection of the most celebrated Songs*, 1763.

Hirsch M. 1355. Songs by T. Attwood, W. Dance, W. Hayes, G. B. Marella, etc.; *circ.* 1800.

Hirsch III. 1001. 'Raccolta di varii pezzi di musica dei più celebri autori', including items by F. Paer, M. Portogallo, A. Tarchi, N. Zingarelli; *circ.* 1810.

Hirsch II. 698. Arias and duets by B. Asioli, N. Mussini, S. Nasolini, F. Radicati, J. Roesler; early 19th cent.

D. 647. a. Songs and dances; early 19th cent. Bound with P. Prelleur, *An Introduction to Singing*, *circ.* 1785.

Hirsch III. 1013. 'Recueil de divers morceaux de musique et romances pour la guitarre à Mde. de Sanzillon'; early 19th cent.

GASPARO SPONTINI

K. 10. c. 16. Letter; 1831.

SIR ARTHUR SULLIVAN

R.M. 10. d. 3. Letter to Sir H. F. Ponsonby; 1891.

GEORG PHILIPP TELEMANN

I. 353. Manuscript material supplementary to an imperfect set of printed parts from a cycle of 72 Cantatas published in 1748–9, including organ continuo realizations for Cantatas 2–5, 10, 12, 13, 16, 21, 22, 29, 34, 44, 57, 63, 69; mostly 18th cent.

SIR HENRY THOMAS

K. 6. d. 1. Card index of settings (mostly in the British Museum) of Horace, Anacreon, Sappho, etc., with other notes and music.

Bequeathed by Sir Henry Thomas.

ERNEST TOCH

Hirsch M. 1356. a. 'Burlesken', op. 31; 1923. *Autograph.* With a letter to Paul Hirsch; 1925.

TRUMPETERS

Hirsch IV. 1440. (i) Franz I, of Austria: Imperial *Brief* confirming revised conditions of service for court trumpeters and drummers; Vienna, 10 June 1747. *Signed. German.* Together with an *Instruction* relating to the preceding *Brief*; 7 Apr. 1748. *German*;–(ii) Johann Peter Büttner, trumpeter to King Augustus III of Poland: *Lehrbrief* for Johann Christoph Rauch, trumpeter, testifying to his successful completion of training; 23 Oct. 1747. *Signed* by Büttner, with signatures of other trumpeters and drummers of the King of Poland. *German.*

GIUSEPPE VERDI

Hirsch II. 920. 'Rigoletto'; mid 19th cent. Full score.

Hirsch II. 924. 'Der Troubadour'; 19th cent. Full score. *German* words.

CORNELIS VERDONCK

E. 1476. Magnificat for five voices; 19th cent. *Copy,* in score, from the edition of 1585.

GEORG JOSEPH VOGLER

Hirsch 5353. 'Beispiele zu dessen Handbuch der Harmonielehre und Generalbass'; early 19th cent.

WANDERING MINSTRELS, THE

K. 6. e. 1–7. Three albums of programmes, drawings, press cuttings, etc.; 1860–98. With a manuscript register of members and receipts, a catalogue of the music library, and other material.

GOTTFRIED WEBER

R.M. 25. d. 6. Letter to the Prince Regent; 1817.

ALBERTUS WERL

K. 3. m. 21. Lute pieces, in Michelangelo Galilei, *Il primo libro d'intauolatura di liuto*, 1620. *Autograph.*

JOHN CLARKE WHITFELD

H. 1275. b. Letter to the publisher, D'Almaine; n.d. Bound in a copy of Clarke's *Twelve Vocal Pieces*, [1816].

JOSEPH WILDE

e. 284. b. (10*.) '12 Walzer für den Carneval', for piano; 1815.

JOHANN RUDOLF ZUMSTEEG

R.M. 25. f. 3. Letter to George III; 1799.

Note: A card index of *autograph* signatures and dedications on printed music is kept in the Music Room.

MUSIC MANUSCRIPTS ON LOAN TO THE MUSIC ROOM

THE MADRIGAL SOCIETY MANUSCRIPTS. A large collection of part-books, etc., of madrigals; late 16th–19th cent. Card index in progress. Madrigal Society G. 9–15, 16–20, 21–26, 27, 28–32, are part of the group of late 16th–early 17th cent. music manuscripts connected with Edward Paston. See Philip Brett, 'Edward Paston (1550–1630): a Norfolk Gentleman and his Musical Collection', *Transactions of the Cambridge Bibliographical Society*, iv, 1964, pp. 51–69.

Deposited on loan by the Madrigal Society in 1953.

INDEX

Note. Music Room press-marks are followed by page references to this handlist in square brackets.

Abbey Glee Club. E.205.p,q; H.1202.jj, kk,ll.[*p.*87].
Abel (Karl Friedrich). 54194.
Acuña (José Francisco). Eg.3288.
Adams (Thomas). 41570.
Agazzari (Agostino). Eg.3665.
Agresta (Agostino). Eg.3665.
Aiblinger (Johann Kaspar). Hirsch III. 595.[*p.*87].
Alard (Delphin). Hirsch IV.1455.[*p.*89].
Albanese (Égide Joseph Ignace Antoine). Hirsch III.1010.[*p.*96].
Albéniz (Isaac Manuel Francisco). Loan 48.13/1.
Albinoni (Tommaso). 38036.
Albrechtsberger (Johann Georg). 38070.
Alcock (*Sir* Walter Galpin). 50756; Eg.3097 A.
Aldrich (Henry). 38648; 39572; 39868; 50859; Eg.2960; K.7.e.2.[*p.*87].
Alison (Richard). K.7.e.2.[*p.*87]; Hirsch M.1353.[*p.*93].
Alkan (Charles Henri Valentin). Hirsch IV.1455.[*p.*89].
Allitsen (Frances). 50849 N.
Ana (Francesco d'). Eg.3051.
Anerio (Felice). 38555-9; Eg.3665.
Ansermet (Ernest). 52256; Eg.3304.
ApIvor (Denis). 53739-66.
Ariosti (Attilio). 38036.
Arkwright (Godfrey Edward Pellew). 50852.
Arnaud (Étienne). Hirsch IV.1455.[*p.*89].
Arnaud (Yvonne). 52256.
Arne (Thomas Augustine). 38188; 39957; 46122; 50896; 54194.
Arnold (Samuel). 40636.
Arriaga y Balzola (Juan de). 42181 D; 43796.
Asioli (Bonifacio). 41094; Hirsch II.698. [*p.*97].
Asola (Giovanni Matteo). 39815.
Astorga (*Baron* Emanuele d'). 39765-6.

Atkins (*Sir* Ivor). 50757.
Attwood (Thomas). Hirsch M.1355. [*p.*96].
Auber (Daniel François Esprit). Eg.3290; K.6.e.2.[*p.*87].
Aubert (Louis). 50505.
Austin (Frederic). 52364; Eg.3304.
Ayrton (William). 52334-47 *passim.*

B. (M). 37772 Q.
Babell (William). 38188; 47446.
Baccusi (Ippolito). Eg.3665.
Bach (Carl Philipp Emanuel). 38072; 39815; 45183; 47843; K.10.a.28.[*p.*87].
Bach (Johann Christian). Eg.3685-8.
Bach (Johann Sebastian). 38068; 38070; 38072; 40636; 41629; 41635; 47839; 50996; Eg.3666; K.10.a.31.(5.).[*p.*93].
Bach (Wilhelm Friedemann). 50115.
Bach (Wilhelm Friedrich Ernst). 39845.
Bache (Francis Edward). 54193.
Bachelor (Daniel). 38539.
Bacilly (Bénigne de). K.1.d.25.[*p.*87].
Baines (William). 50211-38.
Balbi (Lodovico). Eg.3665.
Balfe (Michael William). 43377 E.
Balmani-Naldi (Adèle). Hirsch III.627. [*p.*87].
Bamberg. 50126.
Banks (*Sir* Joseph). Eg.3009 D.
Bannister (John). 47446.
Bantock (*Sir* Granville). 50758; 52364; Eg.3097 A; Eg.3304; Loan 48.13/2.
Baptist. *v.* Draghi, Lully.
Barbirolli (*Sir* John). 52364.
Barnby (*Sir* Joseph). 50759 A,B; D.123.f. [*p.*92].
Barnett (John Francis). 48596.
Barrett (John). 39569(?); 41205; 47446; 47846(?); 49599; 52363.
Bartholomew (Ann S.). 41572.
Bartholomew (William). 47859.
Bartók (Béla). 50496; 51023 A–C; 52256.

99

Bartolini (Orindio). Eg.3665.
Basili (Francesco). Eg.3019.
Bassano (Agostino). Eg.3665.
Bates (John). 38783; 39556.
Bates (Thomas). 38783; 39556.
Bateson (Thomas). Eg. 3665.
Bati (Luca). Eg.3665.
Batta (Alexandre). Hirsch IV.1455. [p.89].
Batta (Laurent). Hirsch IV.1455.[p.89].
Batten (Adrian). 39868; K.7.e.2.[p.87].
Battishill (Jonathan). 50894.
Bax (Sir Arnold). 49602; 50173-81; 52256; 52364; 53709 I; 53735; Loan 48.13/2; Loan 53; Loan 56.
Beczwarzowsky (Anton Franz). R.M.15.a.13.[p.88].
Bedford (Herbert). 48596.
Beecham (Sir Thomas). 52364; Eg.3304; Loan 48.12.
Beethoven (Ludwig van). 38069-71; 38794 H; 41295 P; 41628; 41630-1; 41776; 46135(?); 46839 L; 47851-2; 48590 G; 50896; 52337 B; 52347; Eg.3097 B; Loan 4.21,518-21; Loan 48.13/3.14; Hirsch M.1345; Hirsch 2324; Hirsch 5121.[p.88].
Bellasio (Paolo). Eg.3665.
Belli (Girolamo). Eg.3665.
Bellini (Vincenzo). 38069; 50828; Hirsch II.46; Hirsch M. 1346.[p.88].
Bencini (Pietro Paolo.). 38036.
Benecke (Marie). 41573; Eg.3094.
Benedict (Sir Julius). 37781-3; 48596.
Benevoli (Orazio). Hirsch IV.692.[p.88].
Benjamin (Arthur). Loan 48.13/3.
Bennet (John), madrigalist. 38546; 38554-9; 39815.
Bennet (John), organist. 39868.
Bennet (Thomas). 39868.
Bennet (Sir William Sterndale). 40881; 45909; Eg.3097 B; Loan 4.Supplement 4; Loan 48.13/3; D.123.e.[p.92].
Benoit (Peter). 39255 I.
Beramendi (——). Eg.3288-9.
Berg (Alban). 52256.
Berkeley (Lennox). 52256; 52464 C.
Berlioz (Hector). 38650 G; 47602; 47843; Loan 48.13/4.
Bernabei (Ercole). Hirsch III.1116.[p.96].
Berners, Lord. v. Tyrwhitt-Wilson.
Bertani (Lelio). Eg.3665.
Bevilacqua (Matteo). 47777.
Bianciardi (Francesco). Eg.3665.
Billingham (Edward R.). 41570.

Birche (Thomas). 38783; 39556.
Bishop (Sir Henry Rowley). 38555-9; 50845; 50849 C; 50896.
Bishop (John). A.1231.p.[p.95].
Blake (Edward). 39572.
Blancou (V.). Hirsch IV.1455.[p.89].
Blankenburg (?Quirijn van). 39569.
Blanquin (——). 48346.
Blechynden (Richard). 45580.
Bliss (Sir Arthur). 50849 J; 52256; 52364; Eg.3770; Loan 48.13/4.
Blow (John). 39572; 39868; 41205; 47845; 50859-60; 52363; 54194; Eg. 2959-60; Eg.3767.
Blumenthal (Jakob). Hirsch IV.1455. [p.89].
Boccherini (Luigi). h.42.n.[p.88].
Boehm (Theobald). 39861; Hirsch IV. 1455.[p.89].
Boëly (Alexandre Pierre François). Hirsch IV.1455.[p.89].
Bologna (Luigi da). 50185.
Bond (?Carrie Jacobs). 50849 N.
Bond (G. Herbert). 50849 N.
Bonoldi (Francesco). Hirsch IV.1455. [p.89].
Bononcini (Giovanni). 38036; 38189; 39549; 39907; 47446; 49599; Eg.2961.
Borchgrevinck (Melchior). Eg.3665.
Borodin (Aleksandr Porfirevich). Eg. 3087.
Boroni (Antonio). 50185.
Borren (Charles van den). 47216.
Bottesini (Giovanni). 46843.
Bottrigari (Ercole). Hirsch 5234.a.[p.88].
Boughton (Rutland). 50529; 50960-51012; 52256; 52364-6; Eg.3304.
Bourne (J.). 37999.
Bouth? (Monsieur ——). Hirsch M.1347. [p.88].
Boyce (——). K.7.e.2.[p.96].
Boyce (William). 39572; 47860; 50890; Eg.2964.
Braham (John). 38071; 52335-6.
Brahms (Johannes). 40730 B; 41628; 41866; 46861; 47841 H; Loan 48.13/5.
Breslau. Hirsch IV.1068.[p.89].
Brewer (Sir Alfred Herbert). 50760-1.
Brewer (Thomas). 38546; 38555-9.
Brian (Havergal). 51056-65; 54212-3.
Bridge (Frank). 52256.
Bridge (Sir John Frederick). 38783; 50762; R.M.14.c.21.[p.88]; D.123.f,k. [p.92].
Britten (Benjamin). 52256.

Broadley (Robert). H.1501.(3.).[p.88].
Brocus (Nicolaus). Eg.3051.
Broschi (Carlo). v. Farinelli.
Bruch (Max). Loan 48.13/5.
Bruckner (Anton). Eg.3159.
Bruinincks (Hamel). 39569.
Bryan (?Cornelius). 38545.
Bryne (Albertus). K.7.e.2.[pp.87,96].
Buckley (Olivia Dussek). R.M.8.f.16.
    (1.).[p.88].
Bull (John). 39572; 40657–61.
Bumpus (John Skelton). 50202; Eg.
    3093; G.518.a–c.[p.88].
Bumpus (Mary Frances). 50071.
Bunting (Edward). 41508–10.
Burgmüller (Norbert). 41628.
Burney (Charles). 39957; 48345; 52540
    J; Eg.3009 D; Case 45.f.4–8.[p.91].
Bush (Alan). 52464 B.
Busoni (Ferruccio). Eg.3304; Loan 48.13/
    5.
Butt (Clara). 52364.
Büttner (Johann Peter). Hirsch IV.1440.
    [p.97].
Byrd (William). 38539; 39550–4; 39572;
    41156–8; 47844–5; 50859; Eg.3665;
    Eg.3722; K.2.f.1.[p.88]; K.7.e.2.[p.87].
Byron (William), Lord Byron. 47846.

Caccini (Giulio). Eg.3665.
Caldara (Antonio). 38036; 39922 F.
Caldicott (Alfred James). 49318.
Calista (Lelio). Hirsch III.1116.[p.96].
Callcott (John Wall). 38555–9.
Calvocoressi (Michel Dmitri). 50496–
    505.
Camporese (Violante). 52335–6.
Caproli (Carlo). Hirsch III.1116.[p.96].
Cara (Marchetto). Eg.3051.
Carissimi (Giacomo). 38648; Eg.2960.
Carr (Frank Osmond). 49318.
Carr (Howard Ellis). 50822.
Carse (Adam). h.42.n.[p.88].
Casati (Gasparo). Eg.2960.
Casati (Girolamo). Eg.3665.
Casella (Alfredo). 52256.
Casentini (Marsilio). Eg.3665.
Cassel. Hirsch IV.1068.[p.89].
Catch Club. v. Noblemen's and Gentle-
    men's Catch Club.
Catel (Charles Simon). 38069.
Cavallo (Peter). Hirsch IV.1455.[p.89].
Chaluz de Vernevil (F.T.A.). R.M.14.a.
    21.[p.89].

Chambonnières (Jacques Champion de).
    39569.
Chapel Royal Manuscripts. R.M.23.m.
    1–6; R.M.27.a.1,etc.[p.86].
Chappell (William). 38789; 47216.
Chard (George William). 38069; 50894.
Charpentier (Gustave). Eg.3304.
Charpentier (Marc Antoine). 39569.
Chaynee (Joannes). 41156–8.
Chelard (Hippolyte). Hirsch IV.1455.
    [p.89].
Cherubini (Luigi). 49286; Loan 4.40,582.
Cheshire (John). 44919 S.
Chetwoode (?Robert.) 40657–61.
Child (William). 38539; 39572; 39868;
    50859.
Chopin (Frédéric). 47861 A; 47908;
    Eg.3040.
Church (John). 39572.
Church House Manuscripts. 50888–900.
Cifra (Antonio). Eg.3665.
Clapisson (Antoine Louis). Hirsch IV.
    1455.[p.89].
Clark (Edward). 52256–7.
Clarke (James Hamilton Siree). 44880;
    44919 HH.
Clarke (Jeremiah). 38541; 39565–7;
    39569; 39572; 39868; 47446; 47846;
    52363; Eg.3767.
Clarke (Simon). 39555.
Clarke Whitfeld (John). v. Whitfeld.
Clay (Frederic). 38785.
Clayton (Thomas). Eg.3664.
Clementi (Muzio). 47843; 47854; 47860;
    47862; 48212 O; 52337 A; Loan 48.13/6.
Coates (Eric). 52256.
Cocchi (Gioacchino). 50185.
Cochlaeus (Johannes). 38540.
Coco (M.) 50849 N.
Colasse (Pascal). 39565–7; 39569.
Coleman (Charles). 38783; 39556.
Coleridge-Taylor (Samuel). 41570;
    50763–5; Eg.3096; Loan 48.13/7.
Colonnese (Filippo). 39907.
Comettant (Jean Pierre Oscar). Hirsch
    IV.1455.[p.89].
Conti (Francesco Bartolomeo). 38036.
Cook (Capt. Henry). Eg.2960(?).
Cooke (Benjamin). 38554–9; 50892.
Cooke (Grattan). 50861.
Cooke (Robert). 39572.
Coperario (Giovanni). 39550–4; 40657–
    61; Eg.2971; Eg.3665.
Corelli (Archangelo). 38188; 39565–7;
    39569; 47446.

Corri (Montague). R.M.13.e.3.[p.90].
Corri (Natale). 52540 G.
Cossmann (Bernhard). Hirsch IV.1455. [p.89].
Costa (Luiz). 50187.
Cottrau(Giulio). 50262–74; G.691.b.(19.); G.691.c.(20,22–5.).[p.90].
Coudeno (Giovanni). Eg.3665.
Courteville (Raphael). 52363; Eg.2960.
Cowan (William). Eg.3093.
Coward (Sir Henry). 50766.
Cowen (Sir Frederick Hymen). 50767; 52426; Eg.3304; D.123.f.[p.92].
Cramer (Johann Baptist). 38070–1; 47857; 48212 O; Loan 4.1021; Hirsch IV.1455.[p.89].
Cranford (William). 39550–4; K.7.e.2. [p.87]; K.1.e.9,10.[p.89].
Crescentini (Girolamo). 51014.
Croce (Giovanni). Eg.3665.
Croft (William). 38668; 39868; 40139; 50890; 50892; 52363; Eg.2959; Eg.2965; Eg.3767.
Crosbey (——). 38783; 39556.
Crotch (William). 38070.
Cummings (William Hayman). 47216.
Curci (Giuseppi). 39815.
Curwen (John). 50752.
Czerny (Carl). 38071; 41628.

Dale (Benjamin). 50490–5; Eg.3304.
Dallapiccola (Luigi). 52256.
Dance (William). Hirsch M.1355.[p.96].
Danzi (Franz). 50849 A; Hirsch IV.1144. [p.90].
Darnton (Philip Christian). 52256.
Darwall (John). 50891.
Dauvergne (Antoine). 50144.
Davey (John). 52421.
David (Félicien). Hirsch IV.1455.[p.89].
Davies (Sir Henry Walford). 52364; Eg.3095.
Davis (William). Eg.3768.
Davy (John). Eg.3290.
Day (Charles Russell). 41637–9.
Debussy (Claude). 47215; 47860; Eg. 3304; Loan 48.13/10.
Deiss (Michael). 41156–8.
Delibes (Léo). Loan 48.13/10.
Delius (Frederick). 49602; 50497; 50886; 52256; 52547–9; 52917; Eg.3304; Loan 48.13/10; Loan 54.
Delius (Jelka). 52549; 52917.
Delsarte (François). 43902.
Dent (Edward Joseph). 52256; 52364.

Dering (Richard). 39550–4; Eg.3665.
Deslins (Joannes). 41156–8.
Dibdin (Charles). 38488 A.
Dieren (Bernard van). 49995; 50186; 50498; 50505; 52256.
Dieupart (Charles). 39569; 47446; 49599; 52363.
Doggett (Thomas). 38189.
Döhler (Theodor). Hirsch IV.1455.[p.89].
Dohnányi (Ernst von). 50790–820; 51066–70; Loan 48.13/10.
Dohnányi (Ilona von). 50811–12.
Donato (Baldassare). 38555–9.
Donizetti (Gaetano). Hirsch II.208,212–14; Hirsch M.1346.[p.90].
Dorus (Louis). Hirsch IV.1455.[p.89].
Dowland (John). 38539; 38554–9.
Draghi (Giovanni Battista). 52363(?).
Dragonetti (Domenico). 52335–6.
Drysdale (G. J. Learmont). 46362 H.
Du Caurroy (François Eustache). Eg. 3665.
Dufay (Guillaume). 43736.
Dunhill (Thomas). 52364.
Dunwalt (Gottfried). Hirsch IV.1081. [pp.88–9].
Dupont (Gabriel). 50505.
Durante (Francesco). 48212 O.
Dussek (Jan Ladislav). 50144.
Dvořák (Antonín). 42050; Loan 48.13/11.
Dykes (John Bacchus). D.123.e.[p.92].

East (John). 38783; 39556.
East (Michael). 38546; 38555–9; Eg. 3665.
East (Thomas). 38541.
Eberlin (Johann Ernst). 41633.
Eccles (John). 40139; 41205; 47446; 47846; 49599; 54194.
Edwards (Frederick George). 41570–4; Eg.3090–7.
Edwards (Richard). 38554(?); 52523.
Egerton (Hon. John Grey Seymour). K. 6.e.4.[p.90].
Elgar (Sir Edward William). 41570; 47895; 47900–8; 49602; 49973–4; 50188; 50850 L; 52364; 52525–35; Eg.3090; Eg.3097 A; Eg.3303; Loan 13; Loan 17; Loan 44; Loan 48.13/12; Loan 56/35.
Ella (John). 38488 A.
Elliot (——), of Oxford. 38783; 39556.
Ellis (Alexander John). 41636–8.
Elvey (Sir George Job). R.M.14.d.7. [p.90].
Eremita (Giulio). Eg.3665.

Erlangen. 50122–5.
Erlanger (*Baron* Frédéric d'). Eg.3306.
Ernst (Heinrich Wilhelm). 53722.
Esch (Louis van). 48347.
Evans (Edwin). 52256.

Facy (Hugh). 38783; 39556.
Fago (?Nicola). 38036.
Falla (Manuel de). 52256.
Farinelli. 48346.
Farrant (Daniel). Eg.2971; Eg.3665.
Farrant (Richard). 39868; 52523; K.7.e.
    2.[*p.*96].
Fattorini (Gabriele). Eg.3665.
Federici (Francesco). Hirsch III.742.
    [*p.*90].
Fellowes (Edmund). 52364.
Felton (William). 38188(?); Eg.2970(?).
Fémy (François). Loan 4.90.
Feo (Francesco). 39166.
Ferrabosco (Alfonso), *senior*. 39550–4;
    41156–8; Eg.3665.
Ferrabosco (Alfonso), *junior*. 38783;
    39550–4; 39556; 40657–61; Eg.3665.
Ferrari (Giacomo Gotifredo). 50185.
Ferretti (Giovanni). 38555–9.
Ferrier (Kathleen). 52364.
Festa (Costanzo). 38546; 38554–9.
Field (John). 47855; 47862; Loan 48.13/
    12.
Finger (Gottfried). 39565–7; 41205;
    49599; d.24.[*p.*92].
Fingerlin (Johann Conrad von). 50753.
Fiocco (?Pietro Antonio). 39569.
Fioravanti (Valentino). Eg.3289.
Fisher (Thomas Sympson). 40636.
Flotow (Friedrich von). Hirsch II.231.
    (2.); Hirsch II.232.[*p.*90].
Fogliani (Giacomo). Eg.3051.
Fontanelli (Alfonso). Eg.3665.
Forcer (Francis). 39569; 52363.
Ford (Thomas). 38555–9; 40657–61;
    49977 A.
Forkel (Johann Nicolaus). Hirsch IV.
    1068.[*p.*89].
Formica (Antonio). Eg.3665.
Foster (John). K.7.e.2.[*p.*87].
Foster (Myles Birket). Loan 48.16; D.
    123.f,k.[*p.*92].
Fountains Fragments. 40011 B.
Fradel (Carl). Hirsch IV.1455.[*p.*89].
Franck (César). 52912.
Franz I, *of Austria*. Hirsch IV.1440.[*p.*97].
Franz (Robert). 41635.
Fränzl (Ferdinand). 50144.

Fraser-Simson (Harold). 50151–72.
Frescobaldi (Girolamo). 40080.
Fricker (Peter Racine). 52256.
Friedrich (Fritz). 38071.
Froberger (Johann Jakob). Eg.2959.
Frye (Frederick Robert). 41570.
Fuller (?Robert). 39868.
Fuller-Maitland (John Alexander). 52364;
    Eg.3092.

Gabbiani (Massimiano). Eg.3665.
Gabrieli (Andrea). Eg.3665.
Gafori (Franchino). Hirsch IV.1441.
    [*p.*91].
Gagliano (Marco da). Eg.3665.
Gallo (Giovanni Pietro). Eg.3665.
Galuppi (Baldassare). 50787.
Gardiner (Henry Balfour). 50885.
Gastoldi (Giovanni Giacomo). Eg.3665.
Gaviniès (Pierre). h.210.u.(4.).[*p.*91].
Gayerdell (Mark Anthony). 38783(?);
    39556.
Geminiani (Francesco). 38546; 39957;
    47446; Hirsch III.214.a.[*p.*91].
Gerhard (Roberto). 52256; 52588.
German (*Sir* Edward). 45224 B; Eg.
    3096; Eg.3304.
Gerrard (Jarvis). 38783; 39556.
Gesualdo (Carlo), *Principe di Venosa*. Eg.
    3665.
Gibbons (Christopher). 47845; 50890;
    Eg.2960; K.7.e.2.[*p.*87].
Gibbons (Orlando). 38539; 38554–9;
    39572; 39868; 39922 F; 52287; K.7.e.2.
    [*p.*87].
Gilbird (——). 39868.
Giles (Nathaniel). 50201; Eg.2971.
Gillier (Jean Claude). 39569.
Giordani (Giuseppe). 49376.
Giovannelli (Ruggiero). Eg.3665.
Glazunov (Aleksandr). 50505.
Gluck (Christoph Willibald von). 48590
    K; g.996.b.(12.); Hirsch IV.1152.[*p.*91].
Godefroid (Félix). Hirsch IV.1455.[*p.*89].
Goldschmidt (Otto). Eg.3094–6.
Goldwin (John). 39572.
Gooch (Frederick). 40636.
Goodall (Stephen). 38783; 39556.
Goossens (*Sir* Eugene). 52364; Eg.3304.
Goossens (Leon). 52364.
Gordigiani (Luigi). 41093.
Goss (*Sir* John). 39557; R.M.14.d.14.
    [*p.*91].
Goudimel (Claude). 38541.
Gouge (——). 38188.

Gounod (Charles François). 38057; 38071; 50483 E; Loan 48.13/14.
Graener (Paul). Hirsch IV.1445.[p.91].
Graf (Friedrich Hartmann). 50753.
Grainger (Percy Aldridge). 49602; 50823; 50867–87.
Granville Collection. Eg.2910–46.
Gray (Alan). 50768.
Grebst (W.A.). Hirsch IV.751.[p.91].
Greene (Maurice). 38188; 39868; 43863; 47446.
Gregory (James Lively). 41570.
Gregory (Thomas). 38783; 39556.
Gregory (William). 38783; 39556; 47845(?).
Grétry (André Ernest Modeste). 38070; 47843; 50144; Hirsch III.1010.[p.96].
Grieg (Edvard Hagerup). Eg.3042; Loan 48.13/14.
Grove (Sir George). 39679–80; 42233; 50852; Eg.3091.
Grua (Carlo Luigi Pietro). 37779.
Guglielmi (Pietro Carlo). 37995.
Guillot (Antonin). Hirsch IV.1455.[p.89].
Gumpeltzhaimer (Adam). 38541.
Gundry (Inglis). 52464 B.
Guy (Nicholas). 40657–61.

Haas (Carl). Hirsch IV.1455.[p.89].
Hadow (Sir Henry). 42233.
Hadrava (Norbert). 50139.
Hahn (Reynaldo). 52464 A.
Handel (George Frideric). 38002; 38069; 38072; 38188; 39180; 39569; 39571; 39774; 39868; 39957; 40139; 45102 P; 46122; 47446; 47848; 48596; 50845; 50892; 51019; 54194; Eg.2910–46; Eg.2953; Eg.2970; Eg.3009 E; Loan 48.12; R.M.19.f.10.[p.86]; e.5.w.[p.91]; and see the Royal Music Library [p.86].
Hart (George). 54177.
Hart (Philip). 38188.
Harty (Sir Herbert Hamilton). 52256.
Harwood (Basil). 50769.
Hasse (Johann Adolph). 38188; 39568; 39922 F; Eg.2970.
Hassler (Giovanni Leone). Eg.3665.
Hauptmann (Moritz). Hirsch IV.793. [p.91].
Hawkins (Sir John). L.R.39.a.6.[p.91].
Haydn (Franz Joseph). 38069; 38071; 41094; 44940; 46172 H; 47849; 52622; Loan 4.136–8; Hirsch IV.1060; Hirsch M.1355.[p.91].
Haydn (Johann Michael). 41633–4.

Hayes (William). Hirsch M.1355.[p.96].
Heinrichau. Hirsch IV.1068.[p.89].
Helmore (Thomas). 50895.
Henley (William H.). 53721–2.
Henrion (Paul). Hirsch IV.1455.[p.89].
Henry VIII, of England. 39572.
Henschel (Sir George). 42233; 50183; 50770; Eg.3304.
Herbst (Johann Andreas). 38072.
Herschel (Sir William). 49624–32.
Heseltine (Philip). v. Warlock (Peter).
Heyden (J. van der). Hirsch IV.1455. [p.89].
Hilton (John). K.1.e.9,10.[p.89].
Himmel (Friedrich Heinrich). 38546.
Hindemith (Paul). 52256.
Hipkins (Alfred James). 41636–9.
Hirsch (Paul). [pp.87–98 passim]; Hirsch 5903, etc. [p.91].
Hitzenauer (Christoph). 38072.
Hodges (?Edward). 53709 C.
Hoffman (Ernst Theodor Amadeus). 47843; 47861A.
Hofman (Heinrich Karl Johann). Loan 4.217.
Holborne (Anthony). 38539; Eg.3665; Hirsch M.1353.[p.93].
Holcombe (Henry). 38189.
Hollander (Benno). 53769–70.
Holmes (Samuel). 52536.
Holmes (Thomas). 40657–61.
Holst (Gustav). 47804–38; 48369; 52364; 52915; Eg.3304; Loan 48.13/16; Hirsch M.1348.[p.92].
Hopkins (Edward John). Eg.3092.
Horn (Charles Edward). 50896.
Horner (Burnham W.). R.M.9.d.12. [p.92].
Horsley (Charles). 42233.
Horsley (William). 38546; 38554–9.
Howard (Samuel). 38488 A; Eg.2970.
Hudson (George). 38783; 39556.
Hughes-Hughes (Augustus). 47216.
Humfrey (Pelham). 38648; 39868; 47845; 50859–60; Eg.2960.
Hummel (Johann Nepomuk). 38071; 47843; 47856; Loan 48.13/17.
Humperdinck (Englebert). 38071.
Hünten (Franz). Hirsch IV.1455.[p.89].
Husk (William Henry). 39864.
Hutchinson (Richard). K.7.e.2.[p.87].
Hylton (Jack). 41567 D.

Indy (Vincent d'). Loan 48.13/17.
Ingegneri (Marc Antonio). Eg.3665.

Ireland (John). 52256; 52871–901; Loan 56/36.

Isaac (Heinrich). 38541; 38546.

Isnardi (Paolo). Eg.3665.

Ives (Simon). 38783; 39556; 40657–61.

Jackson (William), *of Exeter.* 50894.

Jackson (William), *of Masham.* 52464 A.

Jacques (Edward Frederick). 41570.

Jadin (Louis Emmanuel). 46396.

Järnefelt (Edvard Armas). 52364.

Jenkins (John). 38783; 39555–6; K.7.c.2. (1.).[*p.92*].

Joachim (Joseph). 38071; 42718; Eg. 3094–6.

Johnson (Robert). 38539; 41156–8.

Jommelli (Nicolò). 39868.

Jones (Henry Festing). 38176–7; 39674 I; 41671; 41677; 50771.

Jones (Robert). Eg.2971.

Jozzi (Giuseppe). 47860.

Jullien (Louis Antoine). 43468.

Karg-Elert (Sigfrid). Eg.3669–70.

Kelly (Michael). 52335–6.

Kelway (Thomas). Eg.3767.

Kemp (Joseph). 50894.

Kennedy-Fraser (Charles). 52364.

Kent (James). 39868.

Ketélbey (Albert William). 41570; g.860. (1.).[*p.92*].

Kidson (Frank). 47216; 50852.

Kindersley (Robert). 38539.

King (Charles). 39572.

King (Robert). 39569; 41205; 52363; Eg.2959; d.24.[*p.92*].

King (William). K.7.e.2.[*p.96*].

Kingelake (William). 38783; 39556.

Kirchner (Theodor). 41628.

Kistner (Friedrich). 41628.

Klenau (Paul von). 52540 M.

Klengel (August Alexander). Hirsch IV. 1455.[*p.89*].

Kodály (Zoltan). 52256; Loan 49/13–28.

Kolisch (Rudolf). 52256.

Křenek (Ernst). 52256.

Kreutzer (Konradin). Hirsch II.488.[*p.92*].

Kruger (Wilhelm). Hirsch IV.1455.[*p.89*].

Krumpholz (Fanny). 49288.

Kücken (Friedrich Wilhelm). 46135; Hirsch IV.1455.[*p.89*].

Kussevitsky (Sergei). 52256.

Lachner (Franz). 41628.

Ladmirault (Paul). 50186; 50499.

Lagarde (N. de). Hirsch III.1010.[*p.96*].

Lambert (Constant). 52257.

Lampe (Johann Friedrich). 39816.

Lanciani (Flavio Carlo). 39907.

Lane (Jane), *afterw. Lady Clement Fisher.* 45850 M(?).

Lanfray Chauftière (Mme. ——). Hirsch M.1347.[*p.92*].

Lasso (Orlando di). 38546; 38555–9; 47844; Eg.3665; A.339.b.[*p.93*].

Latour (——). 47446.

Laurence (John). 38783; 39556.

Lawes (Henry). 53723; K.7.e.2.[*p.87*].

Lawes (William). 38783; 39556; 40657–61.

Le Bègue (Nicholas Antoine). 39569.

Le Cieux (Léon). Hirsch IV.1455.[*p.89*].

Leeman (A.). Hirsch IV.1455.[*p.89*].

Leeves (William). 38541.

Lefébure-Wély (Antoine). Hirsch IV. 1455.[*p.89*].

Legnani (Luigi). 38036.

Leibowitz (René). 52257.

Le Jeune (Claude). 38541; Eg.3665.

Lemans (——). Hirsch III.1010.[*p.96*].

Leo (Leonardo). 39166; 40081; 41094; 48347.

Leoni (Leone). Eg.3665.

Le Strange (*Sir* Nicholas). 39550–4.

Leveridge (Richard). 47860; Eg.2957.

Liapunov (Sergei). 50500.

Liddle (William Henry). 45898.

Liebermann (Max). Hirsch IV.1455. [*p.91*].

Liegnitz. Hirsch IV.1068.[*p.89*].

Liliukalani, *Queen of Hawaii.* R.M.13.f. 11.(1.).[*p.92*].

Lillo (Giuseppe). 41094.

Lilly (John). 38783; 39556.

Lind (Jenny). 43377 A; 45224 Q; Eg. 3095.

Linley (Thomas), *senior.* 38555–9; 39549.

Linley (William). E.1858.cc.[*p.94*].

Liszt (Franz). 38071; 41628; 52311 G; Loan 48.13/18.

Lloyd (Charles Harford). 50772; D.123. k.[*p.92*].

Locke (Matthew). 47845; 50860; Eg.2960.

Loewenberg (Alfred). 48304–11.

Logan (——). 38622.

Long (S.). 39868.

Lotti (Antonio). 38036; 39817; 41094.

Lugg (John). 50201.

Lully (Jean Baptist). 39569; Eg.2963; d.24; Hirsch III.906; Hirsch IV.1692.a.[*p.92*].

Lupo (Joseph). Eg.3665.
Lupo (Thomas). 39550-4; 40657-61; 48590 I; Eg.3665.
Luprano (Filippo de). Eg.3051.
Lustrini (Bartolomeo). 50138.
Lutz (Wilhelm Meyer). 49318.
Luzzaschi (Luzzasco). Eg.3665.
Luzzi (Benedetto). 48348.

MacDermott (Kenneth Holland). 47775.
MacDowell (Edward Alexander). 40728; Eg.3096.
Macfarren (*Sir* George Alexander). 40636; 50773 A,B.
Macfarren (Walter Cecil). D.123.e. [*p.*92].
Mackenzie (*Sir* Alexander). 46912 N; 50774-5; Eg.3305.
Macpherson (Charles). 50776.
Macque (Giovanni de). Eg.3665.
MacVeagh Fragment. 41667 I.
Madrigal Society Manuscripts. [*p.*98].
Mahillon (Victor). 41636-9.
Mahler (Gustav). 49597 B.
Mancini (Francesco). 38036; 40139; Eg. 2962(?).
Manfroce (Nicola Antonio). 41093.
Manna (Ruggiero). 41093.
Manning (William Westley). 47216.
Manuel (Roland). 50505.
Manzoletto (——). 48348.
Marcello (Benedetto). 38070; 38540; 48596.
Marchant (*Sir* Stanley). 50777.
Marella (Giovanni Battista). Hirsch M. 1355.[*p.*96].
Marenzio (Luca). 38555-9; 40657-61; 41156-8; Eg.3665.
Marschner (Heinrich August). 47861 A.
Marsh (W.). 50894.
Marsolo (Pietro Maria). Eg.3665.
Marson (George). K.7.e.2.[*p.*87].
Martin (——). 38188.
Martin (*Sir* George Clement). 50778; D.123.f.[*p.*92].
Martini (——). 38036; Eg.2970.
Martini (*Padre* Giovanni Battista). 39815.
Masi (Giovanni). 50138.
Massenet (Jules). 50483 O; 52425; Loan 48.13/23.
Matteis (Nicola). Hirsch IV.1633.[*p.*93].
Maunder (John Henry). 49595; Eg.3097 A; D.123.f,k.[*p.*92].
Maw (Nicholas). 52464 C.
Maximo (Feliz). Eg.3289.

Maxtime (Thomas). 38783; 39556.
Mayer (Max). Hirsch IV.1455.[*p.*89].
Mayr (Johann Simon). 47776; Hirsch II. 565; Hirsch II.566.[*p.*93].
Mazzoni (P.). 48596.
Meckbach (Wilhelm). Hirsch 5641.[*p.*94].
Mees (J. H.). R.M.12.b.3.[*p.*93].
Méhul (Étienne Henri). 47860.
Meifred (Pierre Joseph Émile). Hirsch IV. 1455.[*p.*89].
Mel (Rinaldo del). Eg.3665.
Melba (*Dame* Nellie). 49977 F; Eg.3305.
Melia (Gabriele). 48348.
Mendelssohn Bartholdy (Felix). 38071-2; 38091 E; 40636; 41570-1; 41628; 46347; 47843; 47858-60; 48597; 52337 A; Eg. 2955; Eg.3094; Eg.3097 B; Loan 4.289, 777,779; Loan 48.13/23; K.10.a.31.(5.); Hirsch M.1349; g.708.[*p.*93].
Mercadante (Saverio). 38071; 48597.
Merulo (Claudio). Eg.3665.
Messager (André Charles Prosper). Eg. 3305.
Meyerbeer (Giacomo). 38071; 50143 F; 52337 A; Loan 48.13/23.
Meyerstein (Edward Harry William). 47843-62.
Milhaud (Darius). 52257.
Millico (Giuseppe). 48347.
Moeran (Ernest John). 52257.
Mogavero (Antonio). Eg.3665.
Moivre (—— de). 47446.
Molinaro (Simone). Eg.3665.
Monari (Clemente). 38036.
Monk (Edwin George). 50897.
Monsigny (Pierre Alexandre). Hirsch III.1010.[*p.*96].
Monte (Philippe de). Eg.3665.
Monteverdi (Claudio). 40657-61; Eg. 3665.
Montgomery (William Henry). 47688.
Montour (H. de). Hirsch IV.1455.[*p.*89].
Moral (Pablo del). Eg.3288.
Morales (Cristóbal de). 41156-8.
Moralt (Peter). Hirsch IV.1455.[*p.*89].
Moretti (Federico). Eg.3288-9.
Moretti (Luigi). 48347.
Morgan (*Dr.* ——). 39565-7; 47446.
Morley (Thomas). 38546; 38554-9; Eg.3665.
Morten Collection. 38068-72.
Moscheles (Felix). Eg.3094; Eg.3096; Eg.3097 B.
Moscheles (Ignaz). 45984; Loan 4.1194; Hirsch IV.1455.[*p.*89].

Mosel (Ignaz Franz von). 38545–6; 38555–7; 38559.
Mosto (Giovanni Battista). Eg.3665.
Mounsey (Elizabeth). 41572; Eg.3094.
Mozart (Constanze). 41628; 47843.
Mozart (Leopold). 41628; 41633.
Mozart (Wolfgang Amadeus). 38070(?); 38072; 41628; 47850; 47861 A; 49973 A; 50139; 50143 F; 50185; 50845; Eg.3097 B; Loan 42; K.6.e.2; e.490.t; Hirsch M.1350; Hirsch M.1351; Hirsch M.1355; Hirsch 5641; Hirsch IV.1449. [pp. 93–4].
Mozart (Wolfgang Amadeus), junior. 41628.
Muffat (George). 39569.
Müller (Louis). Hirsch IV.1455.[p.89].
Mundy (John). 50203.
Mundy (William). 39572; Eg.3665(?).
Munich. Hirsch IV.1068; Hirsch IV.1075.[p.89].
Muris (Johannes de). Eg.2954.
Musgrave (Thea). Loan 4.Supplement 10.
Musical League, The. 49600–3.
Mussini (Natale). Hirsch II.698.[p.97].

Nadermann (——). Hirsch M.1356. [p.94].
Naldi (Giuseppe). 52335–6.
Nanino (Giovanni Maria). Eg.3665.
Nasolini (Sebastiano). Hirsch II.698. [p.97].
Neisse. Hirsch IV.1068.[p.89].
Nelham (Edmund). K.1.e.9,10.[p.89].
Nenna (Pomponio). Eg.3665.
Neukomm (Sigismund von). 48597; Loan 4.804.
Nevile (John). 39555.
Newman (Ernest). 52257; 52364.
Niccolini (Giuseppe). 47777; Hirsch II.687.[p.94].
Nicholls (Horatio). v. Wright (Lawrence).
Niecks (Friedrich). Eg.3095; Eg.3097 A.
Niedermeyer (Abraham Louis). 48596; Hirsch IV.1455.[p.89].
Nijinsky (Vaslav). 47215.
Nin (Joaquín). 52257.
Nissen (Constanze von). v. Mozart (Constanze).
Noblemen's and Gentlemen's Catch Club. [p.94].
Nodari (Giovanni Paolo). Eg.3665.

Notari (Angelo). 46378 B.
Novello (Vincent). 50849 D; K.5.b.8. [pp.94–5].
Nuremberg. 50127–8.

Oakeley (Sir Herbert Stanley). 40636.
Oberhoffer (George). 48596.
Oberthür (Charles). Hirsch IV. 1455. [p.89].
Offenbach (Jacques). 42064; Hirsch II. 690–1.[p.95].
Ogny (Comte —— d'). Hirsch IV.1085. [p.89].
O'Keeffe (John). 38622.
O'Neill (Norman). 53717–20.
Onslow (André Georges Louis). 38058.
Orczy (Baron Bodog). 47220.
Orlandini (Antonio). Eg.3665.
Orologio (Alessandro). Eg.3665.
Osborne (George Alexander). Hirsch IV. 1455.[p.89].
Ottoboni (Antonio). Eg.3022–4.
Ouseley (Sir Frederick Arthur Gore). 41328; 41570; G.518.a–c.[p.88].

P.(N.).39555.
Pacieri (Giuseppe). 39907.
Paderewski (Ignacy Jan). 43377 O.
Paer (Ferdinando). 47776; 48347; Hirsch II.698.[p.95]; Hirsch III.1001.[p.97].
Paisible (James). 39565–7; 39569; 49599.
Paisiello (Giovanni). 37772 L; 48346; 49376; Eg.2966–8; Hirsch III.972.[p.95].
Palestrina (Giovanni Pierluigi da). 38070; 38554; 41156–8; Eg.3665.
Pallavicino (Benedetto). 40657–61; Eg. 3665.
Palma (Giovanni Vincenzo). Eg.3665.
Palmela (——). 48346.
Palomba (Giovanni). 37995.
Paradisi (Domenico). 50138.
Parry (Sir Charles Hubert Hastings). 40730 I; 41570; 42233; Eg.3090; Eg.3305; Loan 48.13/26; D.123.f.[p.92].
Parsons (Robert). 39572; 41156–8; 47844; Eg.3665.
Pasquini (Bernardo). 39674 H; 39907; Eg.2962; Hirsch III.896.[p.96].
Paston (Edward). 41156–8; Madrigal Society Manuscripts.[p.98].
Pattrick (Nathaniel). K.7.e.2.[p.96].
Paxton (Stephen). 38546; 47862.
Pearsall (John). 39549.
Pearsall (Robert Lucas). 38540–63.
Pecci (Tomaso). Eg.3665.

Pedersøn (Mogens). Eg.3665.
Peerson (Martin). K.7.e.2.[p.87].
Pepusch (Johann Christoph). 39569; 40139; 47446; 50359.
Perabo (Johann Ernst). 41628–35.
Peracchini (Giovanni Battista). 48348.
Pergolesi (Giovanni Battista). 38070(?); 41063 M(?); 48346(?); 49519; Hirsch IV.1241.[p.95].
Perugini (Francesco). 41092.
Perugini (Leonardo). 41091–4.
Petridis (Petro). 50505.
Petschke (Hermann Theobald). 42233.
Petter (Gustav A.). Hirsch IV.1455. [p.89].
Philidor (François André). Hirsch III. 1010.[p.96].
Philippo di Fiandra. v. Wilder (Philip van).
Philips (Peter). Eg.3665.
Piccioni (Giovanni). 38555–9.
Pichl (Wenzel). Eg.2966–8.
Pierson (Henry Hugo). G.518.a–c.[p.88].
Pietragrua (Carlo Luigi). v. Grua.
Pigott (Francis). 52363.
Pijper (Willem). 50501.
Pinello (Giovanni Battista). 38540.
Pinsuti (Ciro). R.M.10.a.8.[p.95].
Pitt (Percy). Eg.3301–6.
Pixis (Johann Peter). Hirsch IV.1455. [p.89].
Pixis (Theodor). Hirsch IV.1455.[p.89].
Pleyel (Ignaz Joseph). 50845; Loan 4. 367–70.
Pollarolo (Carlo Francesco). Eg.2961.
Poniridy (George). 50502.
Porpora (Nicola). 41094; 48436.
Portland Papers. Loan 29/333.
Portman (Richard). K.7.e.2.[p.96].
Portogallo (Marco Antonio da Fonseca). 37968; 47776–7; Hirsch III.1001.[p.97].
Posse (——). 39815.
Potter (Cipriani). Loan 4.374–9, 837–40, 1216–8.
Poulenc (Francis). 52257.
Près (Josquin des). Eg.3051.
Preston (Thomas), of Durham. K.7.e.2. [pp.87,96].
Preston (Thomas), junior. K.7.e.2.[p.96].
Preyer (Gottfried). Hirsch IV.1455.[p.89].
Prisco (Gennaro). 50849 N.
Priuli (Giovanni). Eg.3665.
Prokofiev (Sergei). 52257.
Prout (Ebenezer). 50779; Eg.3095.
Puccini (Giacomo). Eg.3305.

Purcell (Daniel). 38189; 49599.
Purcell (Henry). 38189; 38554–9; 38648; 39565–7; 39569; 39868; 40139; 41205; 47446; 47845; 48596; 50859–60; 50890; 52363; 54194; Eg.2956; Eg.2958–60; Eg.2969; Eg.3767; d.24.[p.92]; Hirsch III.472; G.970.[p.95].
Puzzi (Giovanni). 46396.
Pye (Kellow John). 41570.

Quidant (Alfred). Hirsch IV.1455.[p.89].
Quilter (Roger). 54208–10.
Quintiani (Lucretio). Eg.3665.

Rachmaninov (Sergei Vasilievich). Loan 48.13/28.
Radicati (Felice Alessandro). Hirsch II. 698.[p.97].
Rameau (Jean Philippe). Hirsch II.767. (2.).[p.95].
Ramsey (Robert). Eg.2960.
Randall (John). 38188.
Rauzzini (Venanzio). 50185.
Ravel (Maurice). 50360; Eg.3305.
Ravenscroft (Thomas). 38545–6; 39550–4.
Read (Henry). 38783; 39556.
Read (John). 38783; 39556.
Read (Roger). 38783; 39556.
Read (Thomas). 38783; 39556.
Rébel (Francois). Hirsch II.794.[p.95].
Recalchi (Giovanni Battista). Eg.3665.
Reger (Max). 49597 B.
Reggio (Pietro). Eg.2960.
Regnart (Jacques). 41156–8.
Rehfeld (Fabian). 50849 N.
Reicha (Anton Joseph). Loan 4.854.
Reinecke (Carl Heinrich Carsten). 38071.
Reizenstein (Franz). 52589.
Reske (Jean de). 51020 E.
Richardson (Vaughan). 42065; Eg.3767.
Richter (Hans). Eg.3095; Eg.3301–2.
Ries (Ferdinand). Hirsch M. 1352.[p.95].
Rimonte (Pedro). Eg.3665.
Ritson (Joseph). Eg.3778.
Robeson (Paul). 52364.
Robinson (Percy). 49527.
Rockstro (William Smith). 39674 I.
Rode (Pierre Jacques Joseph). 47861 A.
Roediger (Karl Erich). 50122–9.
Roesler (J. Joseph). Hirsch II.698.[p.97].
Rogers (Benjamin). 38539; K.7.e.2. [p.96].
Rogers (Sir John Leman). 38554.
Ronald (Sir Landon). 52364.

Ropicquet (A.). Hirsch IV.1455.[p.89].

Rose (Johann Heinrich Viktor). 37772 L.

Rosenhain (Jakob). Hirsch IV.1455. [p.89].

Rosetti (Francesco Antonio). 47894.

Ross (William Baird). 41570.

Rossello (Francesco). 38540.

Rossetti (Christina Georgina). 40166 R.

Rossi (Abate Lorenzo de). 50138.

Rossi (Salomone). Eg.3665.

Rossini (Gioacchino). 38071; 43970; 45102 E; 48346; 48596–7; 50185; Loan 48.13/29; Hirsch M.1346; Hirsch II.812. [p.95].

Rousseau (Jean Jacques). 47847; Case 26.g.8.[pp.95–6].

Rowland (John). 38189.

Royal College of Music, The. [p.85].

Royal Music Library, The. [p.86].

Royal Philharmonic Society, The. Loan 4; Loan 48.

Rubbra (Edmund). 52590.

Rubiconi (Chrisostomo). Eg.3665.

Rubinstein (Anton Grigorevich). Loan 48.13/29.

Rücker (Manuel). Eg.3288.

Rueth (Marion Ursula). 51070.

Rushforth (Major ——). D.596.aa.[p.96].

Russell (Henry). 48590 E.

Russell (William). 51016–9.

Rüttinger (Johann Casper). 39570.

Sabbatini (Bernardo). Eg.2961.

Sabino (Hippolito). Eg.3665.

Saint-Foix (Comte Georges de). 47216.

Saint-Saëns (Camille). 41340 E; 41487; 53767–8; Eg.3306; Loan 48.13/29; G. 691.a.(25.).[p.96].

Salaman (Charles Kensington). 42110–11; 42501.

Salter (Philip). 40636.

Sances (Giovanni Felice). Eg.2960.

Santini (Marsilio). Eg.3665.

Santley (Charles). 48595–7.

Sarro (Domenico). 38036.

Sarti (Giuseppe). 48346–7.

Satie (Erik). 50505.

Savile (Jeremy). 38555–9.

Scarlatti (Alessandro). 37976; 38036; 39907; 41094; Eg.2962.

Scarlatti (Giuseppe). Eg.3146.

Scheibe (Johann Adolf). Hirsch IV.905. [p.96].

Schell (Joseph Ludwig). Hirsch III.1068. [p.96].

Schietti (Cesare). Eg.3665.

Schimon (Adolf). 46135.

Schindler (Anton Felix). 41628; 46839 L.

Schira (Francesco). 46396.

Schoenberg (Arnold). 52257.

Schreker (Franz). Hirsch II.849.[p.96].

Schrödl (Friedrich Ludwig). 37772 L.

Schubert (Franz). 40636; 41629–30; 41632; 47861 A; 50253; Eg.3097 B.

Schumann (Clara). 38071; 41628.

Schumann (Robert). 38071–2; 41628–9; 49973 A.

Scolari (Giuseppe). 38070.

Scott (Cyril). Eg.3306.

Scott (Emma Moore). R.M.8.k.13. [p.96].

Searle (Humphrey). 52464 C.

Seemann (Adolphe). Hirsch IV.1455. [p.89].

Séjan (Louis). Hirsch IV.1455.[p.89].

Seligmann (Hippolyte Prosper). Hirsch IV.1455.[p.89].

Senfl (Ludwig). 38544; 38546.

Servais (François). Hirsch IV.1455.[p.89].

Séverac (Déodat de). 50503.

Severo (Antonio), da Lucca. Eg.2961.

Seyfried (Ignaz Xaver von). 39815.

Shanne (Richard). 38599.

Shaw (Alexander). K.7.e.2.[p.87].

Shaw (George Bernard). 50662; 52365.

Shaw (Martin). 52366.

Sheehan (Edward Moore). 50483 D.

Shepherd (John). 47844.

Shield (William). 48596; 51015; 52337 A.

Shirley (Joseph). 38783; 39556.

Shore (Sammuel Royle). 47216.

Sibelius (Jean). Loan 48.13/31.

Silas (Édouard). 37956–64.

Simpson (Christopher). 38783; 39555–6.

Simpson (Richard). 52603–7.

Smart (Sir George Thomas). 41771–9; 42225.

Smart (Henry Thomas). 40636.

Smart (Richard). v. Sumarte (Richard).

Smith (John Christopher). 39569; 39957.

Smyth (Dame Ethel Mary). 45934–50; 46857–63; 49196; 52257; 52366; Eg. 3306; Loan 4.Supplement 2; Loan 48.13/ 32.

Somervell (Sir Arthur). 50780.

Sonneck (Oscar George). 50852.

Sontag (Henriette). 38071.

Sor (Fernando). 48348; Eg.3289.

Sorabji (Kaikhosru Shapurji). 52257.

Soriano (Francesco). Eg.3665.

Southgate (Thomas Lee). 38783; 39550–7; 47216; 50781.

Spagnoletti (Paolo). 52335–6.

Spencer (George). 40139.

Speyer (Edward). 42233.

Spohr (Louis). 38071; 47861 A; 48596; Loan 4.922; Loan 48.13/32.

Spontini (Gasparo). 38071; K.10.c.16. [p.97].

Squire (William Barclay). 39679–80; 49527; 50852.

Stadler (Abt Maximilian). 47861 A.

Stainer (Sir John). 41570; 50782; Eg. 3092; Loan 48.13/32; D.123.i,o.[p.92].

Stamitz (?Anton). 49354.

Stanford (Sir Charles Villiers). 41570; 41642; 42233; 45850 B; 53734; Eg. 3090; Loan 48.13/32.

Stanley (Charles John). 38488 A; 39459; Eg.2970.

Steffani (Agostino). 37779; 39815.

Stegall (Charles). 50783 A,B.

Stephen (J. Leslie). 49633–7.

Steuermann (Edward). 52257.

Stevens (Richard John Samuel). 38546; 38555–9.

Stiastný (Johann). 38488 A.

Stiegler (J.B.). Hirsch IV.1455.[p.89].

Storace (Stephen). 50846.

Stradella (Alessandro). 39907; 45882; Hirsch III.1116.[p.96].

Strauss (Johann). 50849 N.

Strauss (Richard). 52927; Eg.3246; Eg. 3250; Eg.3306; Loan 4.Supplement 5; Loan 48.13/33; Loan 49/1–12.

Stravinsky (Igor). 52257.

Streatfeild (Richard Alexander). 47895.

Striggio (Alessandro), senior. Eg.3665.

Strogers (——). 47844.

Strogers (Nicholas). 52523; Eg.3665.

Stroud (Charles). 39572.

Sturt (John). 38539.

Sullivan (——). Eg.2970.

Sullivan (Sir Arthur Seymour). 38071; 41570; 48596; 49318; 49333; 49977 N; 53777–9; Loan 48.13/33; R.M.10.d.3. [p.97].

Sumarte (Richard). 38783; 39556.

Szigeti (Joseph). 52257.

Tailleferre (Germaine). Loan 4.Supplement 9.

Tallis (Thomas). 38539; 38541; 38550; 38554; 39572; 39868; 41156–8; 50859; Eg.3512; K.7.e.2.[p.87].

Tansman (Alexandre). 50504.

Tarchi (Angelo). Hirsch III.1001.[p.97].

Taverner (John). 41156–8; 47844.

Taylor (Edward). 39815.

Taylor (J.J.H.). 40636.

Tchaikovsky (Petr Ilich). 50483 V; Eg. 3246; Loan 48.13/34.

Telemann (Georg Philipp). I.353.[p.97].

Thelwall (John). 38622.

Thibaut IV, of Navarre. 38545.

Thomas (Ambroise). 41567 R.

Thomas (Anthony). 38189.

Thomas (Arthur Goring). 42233.

Thomas (Sir Henry). K.6.d.1.[p.97].

Thomson (George). 38794 H.

Tibaldi (F). 48348.

Tippett (Sir Michael). 52257; 53771; Loan 59.

Toch (Ernst). Hirsch M.1356.a.[p.97].

Tollet (Thomas). 39565–7; 39569.

Tomkins (Thomas). Eg.3665; K.7.e.2. [p.87].

Torri (Pietro). 38036.

Tosi (Pier Francesco). 38036.

Tours (Berthold). D.123.f.[p.92].

Traetta (Tommaso). 39815; 50185.

Tregarthen (William Coulson). 40636.

Tregian (Francis). Eg.3665.

Trento (Vittorio). 47777; 48347.

Trickett (Arthur). 41570.

Tromboncini (Bartolomeo). Eg.3051.

Tucker (William). 47845.

Tudway (Thomas). 39868; 50860.

Turco (Giovanni del). Eg.3665.

Turina (Joaquín). 52257.

Turle (James). 39752.

Turner (William). 47845; 50860.

Twining (Thomas). 39929; 39936.

Tye (Christopher). 38554–9; 39572; 47844.

Tyrwhitt-Wilson (Gerald Hugh), Lord Berners. 52256.

Urban (Florian). 50139.

V.(J.). 37772 U.

Vaet (Jacob). 41156–8.

Valcampi (Curtis). Eg.3665.

Valentine (Robert). 38531; 54207.

Valmarano (Girolamo). Eg.3665.

Vanbrughe (George). 39549.

Varotti (Michele). A.339.b.[p.93].

Vaughan Williams (Ralph). v. Williams (Ralph Vaughan).

Vecchi (Orazio). 40657–61; Eg.3665.

Vecchiotti (Luigi). 49375.
Venosa, *Principe di. v.* Gesualdo (Carlo).
Venturi (Stefano). Eg.3665.
Verdi (Giuseppe). 48596; Eg.3097 B;
   Hirsch II.920; Hirsch II.924.[*p.97*].
Verdonck (Cornelis). Eg.3665; E.1476.
   [*p.97*].
Veress (Sándor). 52257.
Vernon, Baron. *v.* Warren (George).
Verroust (Stanislas). Hirsch IV.1455.
   [*p.89*].
Vetter (Heinrich Ludwig). 41138.
Victoria (Tomás Luis de). 41156–8.
Violone (Giovanni del). Eg.2961.
Viret (Frédéric). Hirsch IV.1455.[*p.89*].
Viviani (Giovanni Bonaventura). 39907.
Vogel (Vladimir). 52257.
Vogels (H.S.A.). 43469–70.
Vogler (*Abt* Georg Joseph). 41634;
   Hirsch 5353.[*p.98*].
Vrutický (Joseph Vlach). Loan 4.Supple-
   ment 1.
Vulpio (?Giovanni Battista). Hirsch III.
   1116.[*p.96*].

Wagner (Richard). 38069; 49973 A;
   Loan 48.13/35; Hirsch IV.1455.[*p.89*].
Wagner (Siegfried). Eg.3306.
Walker (Ernest). 50784.
Wallace (William). Eg.3306.
Walton (*Sir* William). 47898; 52257;
   52384; Eg.3771.
Wandering Minstrels, The. K.6.e.1–7.
   [*p.98*].
Wanless (Thomas). K.7.e.2.[*p.87*].
Ward (John). 38554–9; 39550–4; 40657–
   61; Eg.3665.
Warlock (Peter). 48303; 49995; 50186;
   50505; 52256; 52523; 52904–12; 54197.
Warner (Peter). 38783; 39556.
Warren (George), *Baron Vernon.* 46134–5.
Wartel (Pierre François). Hirsch IV.1455.
   [*p.89*].
Watson (Henry). Eg.3095–6.
Weatherley (Frederick Edward). 49287
   B,C.
Webbe (Samuel), *senior.* 38544; 38555–9.
Weber (Carl Maria von). 38622; 41628;
   41634; 41778; 43468; 47843; 47853;
   47861 A,B; 47862; Eg.3097 B; Loan
   4.961.
Weber (Gottfried). 38070–1; R.M.25.d.
   6.[*p.98*].
Webern (Anton). 52257.
Weelkes (Thomas). 38554–9; Eg.3665.

Weingartner (Felix). Loan 4.Supplement
   3.
Weldon (John). 39549; 39572; 41847;
   47846; 52363.
Wellesz (Egon). 50505.
Werl (Albertus). K.3.m.21.[*p.98*].
Wert (Giaches de). Eg.3665.
Wesley (Charles). 39168 I.
Wesley (John Sebastian). 40636(?).
Wesley (Samuel). 38071; 45102 Y;
   48302; Eg.3097 B.
Wesley (Samuel Sebastian). 40636;
   45498 Q; Eg.3097 B.
West (John Ebenezer). 50785; D.123.f,
   k.[*p.92*].
Whitaker (Frank). 51023 A–C.
White (John). 52363.
White (Robert). 41156–8; 47844.
White (William). 39550–4;40657–61.
Whitfeld (John Clarke). H.1275.b.
   [*p.98*].
Wilbye (John). 38554–9; Eg.3665.
Wilde (Joseph). e.284.b.(10.*).[*p.98*].
Wilder (Philip van). Eg.3665.
Wilkinson (Thomas). K.7.e.2.[*p.87*].
Williams (Ralph Vaughan). 49602;
   50140; 50361–482; 50843; 50862–3;
   51317; 52257; 52287–90; 52383; 52385;
   52601; 52614; 52620; 54186–91; 54214;
   Eg.3251; Eg.3306; Loan 4.Supplement
   6; Loan 48.13/34.
Willis (G.). 38783; 39556.
Windsor Carol Book. Eg.3307.
Windsor (Elizabeth). 42112.
Winterfeld (Karl von). Hirsch IV.1068.
   [*p.89*].
Wise (Michael). 38648; K.7.e.2.[*p.87*].
Withy (John). 38783; 39556.
Wohlers (Heinrich). Hirsch IV.1455.
   [*p.89*].
Wolf (Hugo). Eg.3158–9.
Wolff (Edward). 38070; Hirsch IV.1455.
   [*p.89*].
Wolf-Ferrari (Ermanno). Eg.3306.
Wood (——). 41205.
Wood (Charles). 50786.
Wood (*Sir* Henry). 42233; 52257;
   52366; Eg.3306.
Woodington (Thomas). 38783; 39556.
Woodson (Thomas). 38783; 39556.
Wooler (John Pratt). 47688.
Worgan (John). 38488 A.
Wright (Ellen). 48596.
Wright (Lawrence). 41567 D.
Wrightson (Herbert James). 41570.

Y.(N.).   39555.
Young (William).   38783; 38811; 39556.
Yriarte (Tomás de).   Eg.3289.
Ysaÿe (Eugène).   41570.

Zavertal (Ladislas).   43867; 45102 A;
  47219.
Zavertal (Vaclav Hugo).   43867; 45102
  Q.

Zelter (Carl Friedrich).   38070.
Ziani (Pietro Andrea).   39569.
Zingarelli (Niccolò Antonio).   38070;
  41093; Hirsch III.1001.[p.97].
Zoilo (Annibale).   Eg.3665.
Zumsteeg (Johann Rudolf).   R.M.25.f.3.
  [p.98].
Zweig (Stefan).   51020 M; Loan 42.